KOREA

AN ILLUSTRATED HISTORY

From Ancient Times to 1945

KOREA

AN ILLUSTRATED HISTORY

From Ancient Times to 1945

DAVID REES

HIPPOCRENE BOOKS, INC.
New York

Pictures herein are courtesy of the Korean Information Service (KOIS) and the Independence Hall of Korea.

ISBN 0-7818-0785-9

For information, address:
HIPPOCRENE BOOKS, INC.
171 Madison Avenue
New York, NY 10016

Cataloging-in-Publication Data available from the Library of Congress.

Printed in the United States of America

KOREAN PROPER NAMES

In accordance with general Korean usage, Korean surnames are given first. Exception has been made in the case of personalities already better known by their name in a Westernized form, such as Syngman Rhee.

CONTENTS

LIST OF MAPS

*Tongguk-yo Chido, Map of
Korea reproduced in 1720.*

INTRODUCTION

Koreans call their country Choson, literally "morning freshness" or more familiarly, "The Land of the Morning Calm." The climate of Korea, as we might expect from this indigenous name, is a favorable one; but it should be remembered that the weather from season to season depends on two significant factors.

These two factors are the cold Siberian air that flows south during the winter and the warm monsoon air from the Pacific that affects the shores of East Asia during the summer. Korean winters are therefore cold and dry, but there is much sunshine and little of the damp that so characterizes the winters of northern Europe.

Conversely the summers are hot, with a rainy season in July and August. But although there are sometimes high winds during late August and September, Korea lies just outside the track of the typhoons that regularly affect Japan during this season. Both the spring and the autumn in Korea are tranquil temperate periods, when the full beauty of the country may be seen to its best effect.

The Koreans are an ancient and homogenous people, whose ancestors originally migrated from Central Asia and Manchuria. The Korean language is quite distinct from either Chinese or Japanese, and belongs to the Ural-Altaic language group, which includes Turkish and Mongolian. For many centuries, however, the country's serious literature was written in classical Chinese, and Chinese loan words form about half of the vocabulary. The modern trend is for the substitution of Korean words and phrases for Chinese forms, and, in any case, modern Koreans write in their own phonetic script.

In keeping with the country's separate nationality, Korean history extends back over two thousand years. From the unified Silla kingdom of the seventh century to 1945, Korea was one country. Thus neither the long centuries of domination by Imperial China, when Korea was an independent but tributary state within the Chinese Confucian system, nor the modern annexation by Japan from 1910 to 1945 has affected the feeling that Koreans belong to a distinct people. Neither has the artificial division of Korea between North and South since 1945 removed the fundamental feeling that Korea remains one country.

Despite the country's indigenous name, the history of Korea has been anything but calm, with successive invasions by the Chinese, the Mongols, and the Japanese. Today's division of Korea has added a new dimension to this turbulent past. Consideration of Korea's history is inseparable from consideration of Korean geography and the country's central location in North East Asia. The Korean peninsula extends southwards from the Yalu river, the boundary with China and Manchuria, for some 600 miles; the average width of the country is about 150 miles, although at its narrowest point this width narrows to about 100 miles. The total area of Korea is about 85,000 square miles, including some 3,000 islands and islets, mostly in the south and west. Thus the country is about equal in size to Great Britain or New York State.

Of this total area, the Republic of Korea (South Korea) comprises about 38,000 square miles, or rather less than half. But of

Korea's total population of about 62 million people in 1985, some 42 million live in South Korea, and about 20 million in the Democratic People's Republic of Korea (North Korea). We should also note that several million Koreans live in Manchuria, and another 600,000 in Japan—a legacy of Japanese rule in Korea. A recent phenomenon is the emigration of nearly one million Koreans to the United States, most of them from South Korea.

As both warriors and visitors have often discovered in Korea, the land is mountainous, especially in the north. While these mountains are not very high, rising to over 9,000 feet in the Mount Paektu area on the Chinese border, the central Taebaek mountain range is often composed of the characteristically steep hills that dominated much of the fighting in the Korean War of 1950–53.

From the Taebaek range, hilly spurs and valleys extend westwards, and the South Korean capital Seoul lies in one of these valleys, that of the River Han. To the south of Korea, the hills tend to become more gentle, and here are found the river valleys of the Kum and the Naktong, which are old, historic centers of Korean life and civilization. In northern Korea, the Taedong river basin was another center of Korean antiquity.

Historians have often commented that it is Korea's strategic position, rather than its size or wealth, that has aroused its neighbor's interest. A glance at the map will show that Korea lies at the crossroads of Northeast Asia. To the north, the country has a common frontier along the Yalu River for 500 miles with Manchuria, the northeastern region of China. To the south of the Korean Peninsula, the Japanese home islands of Kyushu and Honshu are about 120 miles away; the smaller Japanese islands of Tsushima in the Korea Strait between the two countries are visible from southeast Korea. To the west of Korea, the tip of China's Shantung Province is about 130 miles from Korean Territory. In the far northeast of Korea, along the Tumen River, there is an eleven-mile border with the Soviet Union.

Korea has thus long been a focus of international contention, as the country is a natural bridge between the continental states of Asia and the maritime powers of the Pacific. Traditionally in these matters, the Japanese have described Korea as "a dagger pointed at the heart of Japan," while the Chinese have seen Korea as "a hammer ready to strike at the head of China." Over the centuries, Koreans have thus seen their fate decided by decisions made outside, rather than inside, their country.

It is a commonplace observation in strategic discussion that Tokyo, Peking, and Vladivostok all lie within 1,000 miles of Seoul. The continuing tension along the Demilitarized Zone (DMZ), which divides Korea and lies within 30 miles of Seoul, underlines these historic and strategic rivalries.

In a wider context it should be stressed that despite all the vicissitudes in their history the Korean people, according to one well-known American scholar and writer, the late George McCune, "have developed a national character with all the accomplishments of a common cultural heritage, language and way of life." Another American scholar, Gregory Henderson, writing in 1968, has noted that Korean history is marked by "exceptional historical continuity."

It is this continuity that underlies our story of Korea.

The Three Kingdoms A.D. *600.*

CHAPTER 1

THE THREE KINGDOMS

According to tradition, the mythical founder of the Korean people was Tun'gunwanggom, who was born of a father of heavenly descent and a woman from a bear-totem clan. The legend asserts that he lived in the third millennium B.C., and that he and his family ruled the Land of the Morning Calm for a thousand years.

Probably most of these tribes from which the Korean people descend originally lived in an area between the Taedong River, in what is now North Korea, and the Liao River in southern Manchuria. It was only much later that the Yalu and the Tumen Rivers became the accepted northern boundaries of Korea.

By about the fourth century B.C., the Korean tribal kingdom of Ancient Choson had emerged in this area between the Taedong and the Liao. The kingdom is so called to distinguish it from Choson, the name later given to the whole of Korea. The society of Ancient Choson was based on a relatively advanced iron technology for its tools and weapons; and a warrior ruling class had already emerged.

Chinese influence in the region was ever-present, and *c.* 108 B.C. the Chinese Han dynasty conquered Ancient Choson and established four commanderies or counties. These units were essentially districts ruled by an administrator appointed by, and

1

responsible to, the Chinese Emperor. The Han conquest was significant in that Chinese influence was to remain the predominant one in Korea. Moreover, from Han times to the modern period, China has remained the foreign country with which Korea has had the closest relations.

This attempt to incorporate what is now northwestern Korea into China was not successful. One by one, the four Chinese commanderies were abandoned in the face of Korean pressure; and by about 300 A.D., three distinct Korean kingdoms had emerged.

These kingdoms were Koguryo, which comprised most of today's North Korea and southern Manchuria; Paekche, based in southwest Korea, encompassing the Kum River basin; and Silla, which included most of southeast Korea and the Naktong Valley. (Silla was to incorporate the Kaya tribes to the west of the Naktong.) These three kingdoms—Koguryo, Paekche, and Silla—then fought amongst themselves with the objective of establishing a single hegemony over the Korean Peninsula.

This was a complex political and military process that took over three centuries. However, the three kingdoms soon achieved a high level of social and cultural development, stimulated by the example of China, where a sophisticated civilization had already evolved. The three kingdoms sent tribute to the Chinese Emperor, and a complicated, feudal society gradually emerged in the Korean kingdoms. Each king was surrounded by a warrior aristocracy and a skilled bureaucracy that ruled over a peasantry, which provided the manpower for incessant military campaigning. Furthermore, there was a serf and slave class at the bottom of this society. The new aristocracy that served the Korean kingdoms was more powerful than its Chinese counterpart, where a meritocracy on the pure Confucian model was more in evidence.

Chinese Influence

In particular, Chinese influence on the Korean kingdoms manifested itself through three developments that have left a permanent mark on Korean society. Most important, perhaps, was the adoption of the Chinese language and its ideograph system for all serious Korean written works. From the time of the early kingdoms to the fifteenth century, therefore, the literary language of Korea was Chinese. The spoken language, however, continued to be Korean.

A second Chinese importation was the Buddhist religion, which with its emphasis on enlightenment and loyalty to the state soon became immensely popular. As Buddhism was an undogmatic religion, it soon quickly absorbed local beliefs and superstitions, and became quickly acceptable to all classes. Many Buddhist temples and shrines were now constructed throughout the Korean kingdoms; perhaps it should be remembered that the word Buddha is not a personal name, but a description meaning "the enlightened one."

A third cultural infusion from China into Korea lay in the learning and social philosophy of Confucius. With its stress on filial piety, on loyalty to the ruler, and on the established order, Confucianism had a major influence on social life and reinforced Korean forms of feudalism. Confucianism, in particular, emphasized the five relationships between king and minister, father and son, older and younger brother, husband and wife, friend and

3

Hunting Scene on the Wall of the Tomb of Dancers (Koguryo 5-6 Centuries).

Remains of Mong'chon Earthen Castle, Seoul.

Gilt Bronze Buddha Triad, 563 (Paekche).

friend. The classic works of Chinese Confucian literature, and a Confucian-based examination system for the recruitment of civil servants buttressed the system. Thus by about 600, the three Korean kingdoms were already run along Confucian lines.

For geographical reasons, the kingdom of Koguryo originally had the closest links with China. But Paekche also played a very important role in the wider dissemination of Chinese culture, for this kingdom had close trading links with China. It was from Paekche that Chinese learning reached Japan.

In view of the fact that China was a more highly developed society than Korea, the influence of Chinese writing and thought is hardly surprising.

But in his authoritative *History of Korea*, Woo-keun Han has written of this period that "the most significant fact is not that Korea adopted Chinese culture in such massive doses but that she managed to retain her own distinctive individuality and to adopt Chinese culture to her own purposes while many other people who came under Chinese influence were completely absorbed into the body of Chinese culture and their own culture ceased to exist."

Silla Victorious

While Chinese cultural influence seeped into Korean life during the fifth and sixth centuries, it seemed as if the political rivalry between the three kingdoms would be won by the northern state of Koguryo. This kingdom not only threatened Paekche and Silla, but also was also able in the early seventh century to repel an attack by the Chinese Sui dynasty. When the Sui, exhausted by

7

its effects to dominate Korea, was succeeded by the Tang dynasty, Koguryo was still able to repel the Chinese between 644 and 659.

But the inter-Korean rivalry was won by Silla. This kingdom had been gradually increasing its political, military, and economic potential. The southeastern Korean kingdom had as its capital the legendary city of Kyongju, where relics of the Silla kings are an outstanding attraction for today's visitors. Kyongju was already a major center of Korean arts and sciences by the seventh century, as it successfully adopted Chinese models of government and social organization to its own purposes. Now Silla displayed a high degree of statecraft as well.

In the late seventh century, Silla came to an alliance with the Chinese Tang rulers with the objective of eliminating its rivals. A Chinese army was sent to Korea, and a combined Tang-Silla force overthrew Paekche (660) and then Koguryo (668). Silla was now supreme in central and southern Korea, and the rule of the unified Silla dynasty is dated from 668.

Chinese ambitions to rule the whole of Korea were thwarted by Silla in 676. A Chinese army was expelled from Pyongyang on the Taedong River in northern Korea, and the invaders sent packing to the Liao River far to the north. Korea south of the Taedong was now ruled as a politically unified country by a confident, powerful Silla. Further north, large parts of the former Koguryo kingdom had passed to the Parhae people during the eighth century. Parhae, which included large areas of what is now known as Manchuria, was reckoned a kingdom of Korean people. At first it posed no threat to the unified Silla kingdom, which now concentrated on rebuilding the country after the wars of the seventh century.

General Yongaesomun of Koguryo, who destroyed the troops of Tang China in 655.

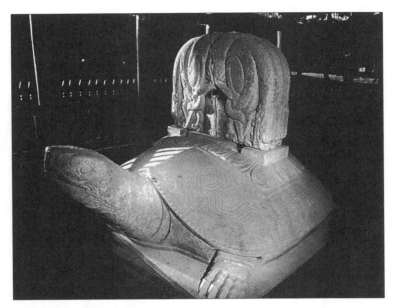

*Tomb of King T'aejong-Muyol (r. 654-661), who led the
unification of the Three Kingdoms.*

Several generations later, in 735, the Chinese formally recognized the kingdom of Silla. The history of Korea had taken an important step forward, for Imperial China had come to terms with a single Korean kingdom.

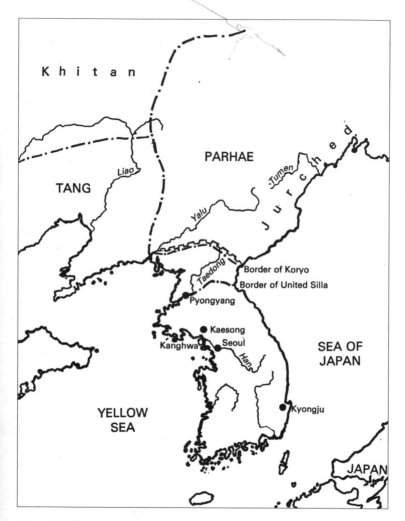

United Silla and Koryo 8th–4th Centuries.

CHAPTER 2

SILLA AND KORYO

 F rom its capital at Kyongju in southeast Korea, the Unified Silla Kingdom extended northwards to the Taedong River and the "waist" of the Korean Peninsula. Under King Kyongdok, who reigned from 742 to 764, Silla reached the peak of its power and prosperity.

Buddhism had been the official religion of Silla for some time, and now, with generally increased wealth, Buddhist monks began to enjoy a position of great power and privilege. It was a period of close Korean contacts with China, and some Buddhist monks went as far as India to obtain Buddhist scriptures. Other Korean traders and artists went to Japan, bringing with them further infusions of Chinese thought and learning. This was the great age of the Tang dynasty in China, but it is recorded that the temples of the Silla capital at Kyongju were as richly appointed as any in China. Royal patronage was an important factor in this outpouring of Buddhist art and architecture.

Near Kyongju, during the eighth century, there were four temples built on To-ham Mountain, which formed a natural barrier protecting the Silla capital from the east: two great Buddhist temples, the Pulguk-sa state temple, and the Sokkuram granite cave temple. These temples remain two of the most perfect and celebrated Buddhist monuments in East Asia. The Pulguk-sa temple was partly

Pulguk-sa Temple.

destroyed in the Japanese invasions of the sixteenth century, but some original stone parts of the temple remain. In particular, the Sokkuram shrine—with its figure of Buddha almost eleven feet high, its domed hall, and its delicate stonework—is a masterpiece of Buddhist art.

These two temples were built at the zenith of Silla's power and prosperity. The Silla royal family sponsored their construction, and the execution of the project was the responsibility of Kim Taesong, who had served King Kyongdok as chief minister.

Main Image of Buddha in Sokkuram, 8th Century.

When he died in 774, the Silla kingdom completed the two temples. Other Buddhist memorials from this Silla period include large rock reliefs, which are relatively numerous, and which still attract worshippers. Buddhist temple bells made in the Silla era include many of the biggest and finest ever made, some over ten feet high.

Korea's Largest Bell, the Bell of King Songdok, 725.

The Confucian Order

During the Silla period, Korea achieved full tributary status within the Confucian international order headed by Imperial China. We have already noted that the Confucian domestic order was dominated by the five personal and family relationships.

In the wider international context, according to M. Frederick Nelson's classic study, *Korea and the Old Orders in Eastern Asia*, "to those accepting Confucian ideology, the world stood as a single unit. Under the aegis of heaven, according to this belief, there existed a pre-established world pattern wherein all things had a definite and proper relationship . . ." In this system, China was the Middle Kingdom, to whose ruler Heaven had given its mandate, to whom Heaven looked for the proper ordering of things. Under Silla, Korea was now to find its own distinctive place in this system.

This family of nations was governed by the same rules as the natural family, and hence under the Confucian familistic system, "a nation's duties and privileges were governed by the same rules that preserved harmony in the family and in society." China's relationship to Korea now became that of parent to son, although after the seventeenth century, this was usually termed that of elder to younger brother. The relationship was "familistic and natural," and not legal in the Western sense, as there were no such concepts as the state and legal sovereignty in the Confucian order.

Korea did not achieve a place within this system until about the seventh century. Previously, the Middle Kingdom had regarded the Korean kings as barbarians to be conquered or manipulated as events dictated. But as Confucian culture came to dominate Korea, its kings came to consider investiture by the Chinese emperor as necessary to their right to rule. Nelson also writes that "Korean rulers showed their respect by sending tribute to the Son of Heaven and accepting from him their investiture, along with gifts and admonitions concerning the preservation of the natural order." Here was a pattern that was to govern Korean relationships with China until the late nineteenth century; it was only in 1895 that Korea became an independent state in the Western sense.

When barbarians or usurpers overthrew reigning Chinese dynasties, Korea gave up its allegiance to the Son of Heaven until the traditional relationship was re-established. When the Mongols conquered China in the thirteenth century, for example, they found it difficult to control Korea without the Confucian family relationship. Force and direct rule had to be employed. On the other hand, the third country of the Confucian system in East Asia—Japan—sometimes acknowledged and then renounced a tributary status in the Chinese Confucian system.

However, despite all its power, its artistic achievement, and its growing status within the Confucian family, the Silla dynasty went into a long, irreversible decline following the golden age of the eighth century.

For this fatal decline, three factors seem to have been responsible. Firstly, the Silla reigning family was plagued by family feuds and quarrels that completely dissipated its energy. Secondly, Silla was gradually threatened by the growing power of the Parhae kingdom to the north. This development helped to erode Silla's military power, so hastening the dynasty's decline. A third and very important reason for Silla's eventual fall was a series of peasant revolts, the inevitable result of misgovernment.

Early in the tenth century, a great rebel leader, General Wang Kon, became powerful in the Kaesong region to the north of the Han River estuary in central Korea. In 918 Wang Kon proclaimed the dynasty of Koryo at Kaesong, his native town. From this nodal point, the new regime could control a number of important strategic routes that linked the south and north of Korea.

After a prolonged political and military crisis, the last Silla king, Kyongsun, decided to abdicate; and in 935, Wang Kon received the formal surrender of this monarch and his government. The local magnates were left undisturbed for the time being; the Silla aristocracy were accommodated; and the new dynasty was further legitimized when Wang Kon married a woman from the Silla royal family.

In this way, Silla was succeeded by Koryo. The second great dynasty in Korean history was now at hand.

The Koryo Dynasty

In line with Chinese custom, the Koreans gave their kings regnal or descriptive titles after their death, and it is by these names that the Korean kings are known to posterity. General Wang Kon thus became known to history as King Taejo—the Korean form of the Chinese expression for "grand progenitor," or founder.

The age of the Koryo dynasty, from whose name derives the Western term "Korea," was an eventful and significant age in Korean history. Following the establishment of regime, and the reorganization of the bureaucracy on more centralist lines, Koryo

19

embarked on a consistent policy of absorbing northern Korean lands that had been in the possession of the Parhae kingdom.

Parhae had been conquered *c.* 926 by the nomadic Khitan people, who then began raiding Koryo territory south of the Tae-dong River. But in a series of planned offensives later in the tenth century, Koryo drove back the Khitan to the line of the lower Yalu River, thus largely establishing the northern borders of Korea as they have remained to this day. Former Korean lands to the north of the Yalu were now considered lost. In the far northeast, Koryo claimed the Tumen River as the Korean border, but the rise of the Mongol Jurched people in this area precluded effective Koryo control.

Eventually, in about 1044, Koryo built a stone defensive wall across Korea from the lower Yalu to the Eastern Sea (or the Sea of Japan). There was continuing instability on the northern borders of Korea; and in 1136, Koryo recognized the suzerainty of the Jurched Chin dynasty that had conquered North China and Manchuria. Over the next few decades, there was comparative calm on Korea's northern borders.

The early Koryo period was characterized by the rise of an aristocratic landed class, the *yangban*, who were to contest the emergence of a strong monarchy. Another source of latent instability was the conflict between the warrior class and the powerful literary caste that provided the bureaucracy. But nevertheless, there were impressive cultural developments during the age of Koryo.

Buddhism was reconfirmed as the state religion and thus received protection and valued privileges from the Court. Many Korean historical works were written, though some of the most valuable of these books did not survive the subsequent Mongol invasions of Korea. However, of great importance in the cultural history of Korea was the first printing of the Buddhist devotional work, the *Tripitaka*. This production in 6,000 volumes was made possible by the carving of 80,000 wooden blocks. Later destroyed by fire, the *Tripitaka* was re-printed, and survives to the present day. Moreover, during the late Koryo period, movable metal type evolved in Korea—several centuries before this technique was discovered in Europe.

An important intellectual development during this period was the evolution of a sophisticated (and revitalizing) interpretation of Confucianism, which stemmed from the thought of the Chinese sage, Chu Hsi. This neo-Confucianism now emerged as the intellectual basis of an opposition movement to Buddhism, for the privileges enjoyed by Buddhist monks were generating resentment throughout Korean society.

But perhaps the most important cultural legacy of the Koryo period lay in the flowering of Korean ceramic art. Under the Silla dynasty, Korean ceramics had already developed from earthenware and ash-glazed pottery to early examples of the distinctive pale-green porcelain known as celadon. Chinese potters, of course, manufactured a wide range of ceramics; but under Koryo, their Korean counterparts concentrated on producing uniquely refined celadons. With their inlaid, incised designs, even the Chinese regarded Koryo celadons as the finest made; the art reached its perfection under the rule of King Injong (1122–46). Many of these treasures have survived and may be seen in the Korean National Museum in Seoul.

Buildings that house the Tripitaka *at Haeinsa Temple.*

Copper-Alloy Type from the reign of King Sejong.

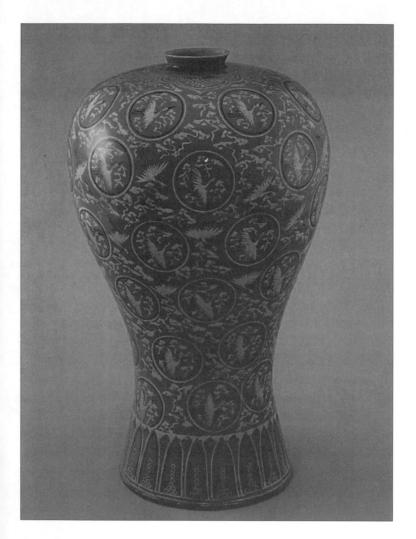

Porcelain Vase with Celadon Glaze (Mid-12ᵗʰ Century).

The Mongol Invasions

The high civilization of Koryo was ended by one of the great catastrophes in Korean history: the Mongol invasions. Korean life was affected for over a century, and the aftermath of this alien incursion led to the fall of the Koryo dynasty.

In 1202 Temujin, or Ghengis Khan, was elected leader of the Mongol horde. By 1215, Eastern Europe had been ravaged, and the Mongols had even conquered China, where they became known officially as the Yuan dynasty. Korea was now affected by Mongol pressure, and at first the Mongols were bought off by tribute.

But in 1231, the Mongols launched a full-scale invasion of Korea, driving down the central mountains to the Han River. The Koryo capital at Kaesong was taken, and heavy tribute exacted. The Korean kings retreated to Kanghwa Island, in the Han estuary. Mainland resistance, however, continued for decades that saw most of the major cities of Korea sacked. Eventually, the country was pacified, and Koreans were even impressed to assist the abortive Mongol invasions of Japan in 1274 and 1281. The failed invasion of Japan, however, marked the Mongol high tide in East Asia.

The Mongols continued to bear down on Korea until the mid-fourteenth century, when the Chinese reasserted themselves under the Ming dynasty. By 1382 the Ming had taken control of Peking, the Koryo kings had removed Mongol officials, and the Mongol era had thus come to an end.

The Koryo dynasty, however, was in a prolonged and insoluble crisis. Removed pro-Mongol officials plotted against the court. There was conflict between Buddhist monks and Confucian intellectuals. The Buddhist monasteries were, in any case, envied for their wealth.

Eventually the fall of Koryo was brought about indirectly, by the ravages of Japanese pirates on the southern Korean coast. General Yi Song-gye gained much esteem by countering these pirates; and in 1388, he seized local power in Kaesong. He then began to implement reforms with the backing of the Confucian elite.

General Yi was proclaimed king in July 1392, so ending the Koryo dynasty. The Yi dynasty would last into the twentieth century, linking medieval with modern Korea, so that there are Koreans still living who were born under the Yi.

Bodhisattva Avalakitesvara (Koryo, 14ᵗʰ Century).

The Eight Provinces of the Yi Dynasty, 14th–19th Century.

CHAPTER 3

KOREA UNDER THE YI

Following his assumption of power in 1392, General Yi Song-gye was recognized by the Supreme Council, the most important body in the Koryo administration. The Council stated that the Koryo dynasty had ended, and that General Yi was now the legitimate ruler of Korea. The new king would be given the same posthumous title as the founder of the Koryo dynasty—Taejo—and it is by this name that posterity knows the first Yi king.

As part of his general policy of reform, King Taejo replaced Buddhism as the state religion with Confucianism. Confucian learning was given priority, and neo-Confucian scholars, well versed in Chu Hsi's doctrines, achieved great influence. These scholar-officials who were recruited by the new king in effect acted as senior royal advisers. The king had an interest in benevolent rule, for he was regarded as possessing the Mandate of Heaven. Many Confucian teaching institutions were set up as part of this policy of establishing a Confucian state.

Most of these Confucian scholar-officials came from the *yangban*, or landed aristocratic class. The term may be used generally to describe this official-landed class or to refer to individuals. The *yangban* had begun to emerge as a class in late Silla times, and had contested the development of a strong Koryo monarchy in Korea, as we have already noted. There were thus good reasons of state why King Taejo now made a determined attempt at land reform. This reform aimed at establishing the royal authority and, at the same time, bettering the living conditions of the ordinary peasant and small tenant farmer.

With the support of many of his Confucian officials, Taejo decreed that all land was to be held by the state and reapportioned. Royal officials could only hold land when they were actually in office. The general thrust of King Taejo's policy was thus aimed at creating a reformed, centralized monarchy based on the ascendancy of the king over the *yangban* landed magnates.

Founding the Dynasty

King Taejo moved to establish his authority in a number of other ways. Early in his reign, he reaffirmed his country's traditional tributary relationship with the Ming rulers of China. The Chinese Emperor approved a new name for Korea—Choson—which had been the title of the earliest Korean state. It was in this way that Korea acquired its modern name of the Land of the Morning Calm. The dynasty founded by King Taejo is thus often called Choson by Korean historians, although in the West it is generally known as the Yi.

Of great importance was King Taejo's decision to transfer the Korean capital from Kaesong, with its Koryo associations, to Hanyang (later Seoul)—a hilltop fortress site in the lower valley of the Han River and near the Yellow Sea. Taejo had very early decided to move from Kaesong, but it was not apparent at first that Seoul would be the choice. One of the critical elements in the

Lifestyle of the Yangban during the Yi Dynasty.

final decision over the new Yi capital was the ancient Oriental science of Geomancy.

This pseudo-science, which had great influence in China, Japan, and Korea, stemmed not from Confucianism but rather from the Chinese religion of Taoism. Essentially, Geomancy taught that the physical outlines of a landscape had great influence on the people living there. But these "marks of a propitious character" had to be interpreted by learned intermediaries, especially as "wind" and "water" elements had to be carefully assessed, as well as those of male and female.

Although King Taejo was disposed to establish his new capital in southern Korea, a Buddhist monk associated with him, Mu-Hak believed that the vital signs indicated Hanyang. Here was an attractive site guarded by a northern mountain (Pugak-san) and a southern mountain (Nam-san). After some deliberation, the preference of Mu-Hak proved decisive and the king adopted Seoul as his capital in about 1395. The site was in any case in the strategic center of Korea, with good access to both the north and the south of the country.

The government thus moved to Seoul, as it became known, and new palaces were built, including the Kyongbok Palace in the center of the site. This palace became the main seat of royal administration. Apart from a few short periods, Seoul was now to remain the capital of the Yi kings through all the vicissitudes of the next five centuries.

Yet another historic administrative development initiated under King Taejo and his immediate successors was the permanent consolidation of northeast Korea as an integral part of the country. To be sure, the Koryo dynasty had claimed the northern

Kungjongjon, the Throne Hall in Kyongbok Palace.

border of the upper Yalu and Tumen Rivers in this region, but the Koryo kings had been unable to conquer the nomadic tribes of the area and bring the region into the Korean administrative structure.

With King Taejo, a determined effort was begun to solve this problem. Under Taejo's grandson, King Sejong (reg. 1418–50), the Korean northeast up to the line of the Tumen River was brought under royal control. Garrison towns were set up, civil officials moved in, and immigration from southern Korea was encouraged. And so to this day, the Tumen River remains the northeastern border of Korea.

Another lasting administrative measure of the early Yi kings was the division of Korea into eight major provinces. In later years, these provinces were further divided into northern and southern parts. But the main provincial boundaries have survived into the present.

In each of these new provinces, the Yi kings appointed an administrator, and beneath him were created magistrates with wide executive powers. A military headquarters was set up in each province staffed with army and, sometimes, naval officers. In the northern provinces of Pyongan and Hamgyong, for example, army officers were in control. But in the southern maritime provinces of Kyongsang and Cholla, whose coasts were affected by Japanese piracy, there were sometimes two naval commanders in the provincial military command.

Confucian Government

The centralized Confucian system of government that was created by the early Yi kings in the first century of their rule was to

Tomb of King Sejong.

survive, surprisingly unchanged, into the nineteenth century. Essentially this structure was based on classical Chinese Confucian lines adapted to Korean conditions, and thus a strict hierarchy was an integral part of the system. It must be remembered that the Confucian cultural legacy remains strong, even in today's Korea.

At the pinnacle of government was the king who, like the Chinese Emperor, claimed the divine Mandate of Heaven. The king's authority was absolute and hereditary, for in the Confucian view his government brought about harmony between divine and human activities. Chinese Confucianism held that a ruler could be overthrown if the Mandate was violated by an unjust Emperor. In Korea, this teaching was modified to assert that even a tyrannical ruler could not be overthrown, although in practice Korean kings were deposed or murdered.

The king was surrounded by a mystique and protocol that proclaimed his divine origins. Immediately below the king were the Royal Secretariat and the State Council, which supervised six ministries. These six ministries were concerned with Justice, Personnel, Public Works, Revenue, Rites, and War. Under the Yi, the State Council was soon to lose its supervisory functions, and the ministries were put under the king's direct control. The Council then became advisory only.

An important supervisory part of this government lay in the three Censorate offices. One was known as the Office of the Inspector-General and another as the Office of the Censor-General. The third was the Office of Special Counselors, which advised the king on matters connected with the Confucian classics and their relevance to government.

Confucian Scholars at Sungkyunkwan, or the National
Confucian Academy of the Choson.

Serious criminal offences were dealt with by Royal Guards, who also functioned in cases of threats to the king and to national security in general.

According to the Korean historian, Woo-keun Han, who has described the system in detail, this basic administrative structure was set up during the reign of King Taejong (1400–18), who was King Taejo's son. The laws that governed the system were then duly codified and completed by about 1470.

The essence of the system lay in the stratified bureaucracy with its exclusive relationship between officialdom and the literate *yangban*, aristocratic caste. The bureaucracy encompassed nine grades, each grade subdivided into four, so making a class with thirty-six ascending divisions. As promotion into the upper levels was extremely difficult, the Korean government was a relatively tiny elite that, in practice, perpetuated itself from generation to generation.

The power of this elite was further concentrated by the practice of senior officials holding several posts at the same time. This pluralism further increased the centralization of the system.

In line with Confucius's teachings, which exalted learning and especially literary scholarship, civil servants were held in greater regard than the military. But this demarcation was not always observed, as civil officials sometimes held military or naval rank. However, under the Yi kings it was generally the civil officials of the administration that held the senior policy-making positions.

Inherent in the Yi government was the device that allowed relatively junior officials to present petitions to the king—a method also used by some Confucian intellectuals to see that national policy followed the precepts of the Sage. Commoners could also appeal to the king, but in general these methods did not influence policy. The Yi administration thus remained both autocratic and the preserve of the *yangban* class.

Underwriting the system was the Confucian examination system that was apparently applied with greater strictness under the Yi than under earlier Korean dynasties. But the very complexity of the system turned it into an elaborate screening process that continued to emphasize *yangban* ascendancy. Although there were three examinations—civil, military, and technical—the civil division was of course the most important.

In this category, there were two subdivisions, higher and lower, and the emphasis in both divisions was on the Confucian classics and literature. In the final, higher examination there were three stages respectively held in the provinces, in Seoul, and before the king. Successful candidates were able to serve in all senior administrative posts, a great honor.

The emphasis on hierarchy and status in the Korean government was but a reflection of the firm divisions in society under the Yi dynasty. At the pinnacle lay of course the *yangban*, who inherited both power and wealth. Then came the *chungin*, a small middle class of minor officials. Below them were the *sangmin* (common people) who were largely farmers and thus formed the majority of Koreans. Lastly we find the *chonmin*, a menial class of slaves and generally underprivileged persons.

The Confucian system meant that there was an intense emphasis in the upper reaches of society on learning, which meant, in practice, the study of the Chinese Confucian classics. Familiarity with these classics was the avenue to power and prestige.

Social distinctions were strict, and inter-marriage between classes virtually prohibited. There was an inherent Confucian prejudice against commerce and business that affected both Korean domestic and international trade. This bias against commerce reflected the Confucian precept that for an individual to change his status—for example, by the accumulation of wealth— was abhorrent to society and even to heaven itself.

Thus although the Confucian legacy in Korean life and government emphasized national continuity and stability, it also gave to society a rigidity that even the reforming ambitions of the early Yi kings were unable eventually to overcome.

Cultural Achievements

A high level of cultural achievement was promoted by the early Yi kings, and in particular by King Sejong. The king was a strong believer in the Confucian precept that the study of literature and history was the path to the achievement of individual and collective virtue. This notable reign in the first half of the fifteenth century was also characterized by the development of new ideas in music, medicine, astronomy, and other sciences.

Sejong gave practical effect to his innovative ideas by creating a royal research institute, the "Hall of Talented Scholars" (*Chiphyonjon*). The institute was modeled on Chinese examples, and compiled textbooks and instructional manuals on the Korean arts and sciences, besides providing tutors for the Korean royal family.

The historic cultural achievement of King Sejong's reign, which seems to have been the personal inspiration of the king,

Water Clock invented during the reign of King Sejong.

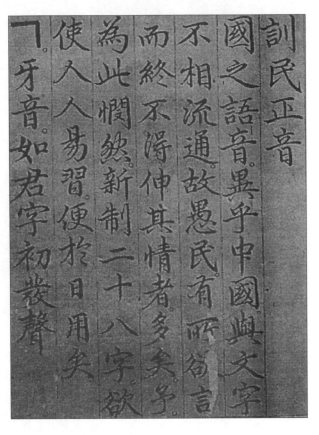

訓民正音

國之語音。異乎中國。與文字
不相流通。故愚民有所欲言
而終不得伸其情者多矣。予
為此憫然。新制二十八字。欲
使人人易習。便於日用矣。
ㄱ。牙音。如君字初發聲

The Text of Hunminjongum (Hangul).

was the promulgation in 1446 of a Korean phonetic alphabet with 28 letters. This was officially called *Hunmin chongum*, "Correct sounds for the people," and became generally known as *Hangul*. Prior to the development of *Hangul*, the only effective written language in Korea was classical Chinese, which was known as *Hanmun*.

Before the promulgation of *Hangul* in 1446, attempts had been made, as in the Idu system, to adapt spoken Korean speech into Chinese characters. But the Chinese and Korean languages were structurally unrelated. This fact—in particular, because Chinese was an ideographic or sign language, while Korean was phonetic—made it enormously difficult for Chinese characters to represent Korean speech. *Hangul* transformed the prospects of the Korean language, for its 28-letter phonetic alphabet could be learnt in a few hours. A premium was thus placed on literacy, as *Hangul* was much easier to learn than Chinese with its thousands of sign-letters.

However, many Confucian scholars objected to *Hangul*, and Chinese remained the language of serious literature, of official administration, and of polite *yangban* society. The Chinese cultural heritage thus remained predominant in Korea, in much the same way as Latin remained the official language in Western Europe at the close of the Middle Ages, when individual European countries were developing their vernacular languages. Moreover, although the Yi court continued to promote *Hangul*, the forces of tradition were on the side of Chinese as a literary language. The phonetic alphabet thus came to be regarded as an inferior usage, and in effect was reserved for popular prose romances and other such works until the increasing modernization of Korea at the end of the nineteenth century.

With the development of general literacy in Korea in the present century, *Hangul* has now come into universal use. Many of the Chinese loan words in Korean have been turned into *Hangul*, and Chinese ideographs or signs are increasingly retained only for technical terms or proper names.

The visual arts flourished as well under the early Yi kings. There was a revival of Korean painting, which now advanced from its Buddhist or religious preoccupations and concentrated on secular, non-religious themes.

As part of this development, professional artists turned to portraits and landscapes, and their work became recognizably Korean in terms of content and technique. These professional painters often worked for the Yi Court and the royal family. Less professional artists, who were often literary men and poets, turned to scroll painting and calligraphy—a form that remained popular with Koreans down the centuries.

Thus in calligraphy, as in the wider artistic field, Korean artists under the early Yi dynasty outgrew their original Chinese models and began to develop their own naturalistic modes of expression. During the early Yi period, therefore, a Korean tradition began evolving in the arts that would continue to develop for the remainder of the dynasty's long life.

Korean ceramics under the Yi, while not so accomplished as those of the Koryo period, were still prized. The earlier demand for the distinctive green Koryo celadons seems to have declined in favor of a highly perfected white porcelain characteristic of the early Yi period.

"Ssirum" or *"Korean Wrestling"* by Kim Hong-do.

"Sage Contemplating the Water" by Kang Hui-an (1419–1464).

White Porcelain Faceted Bottle.

Yangban Rivalry and Reassertion

The paternalistic administration of King Sejong, the inventor of *Hangul*, was probably a golden age. Although the cultural achievement remained, Sejong's reign was followed by a prolonged period of feud and rivalry within the court and the *yangban* class.

This period of instability was characterized by a reassertion of the power of the traditional aristocracy, the *yangban*. The early Yi kings had embarked on a policy of land reform and had attempted to curtail the privileges of the *yangban*. An attempt was made to restrict the holding of estates by these nobles only when they held office. Both King Sejo (1455–68) and King Songjong (1469–94) attempted to continue this policy.

As the *yangban* class continued to hold very real power through their monopoly of office, however, they were able to resist the royal policy and to continue to expand their estates, known as *nongjang*. The *yangban* put pressure on a series of kings to accept their privileges and, at the same time, continued to improve their position by a series of extralegal devices. One such device was the removal by the landlords of tenants from the official tax lists, so weakening the royal treasury. Another was the exclusion of *yangban* tenants from the draft or conscription rolls, so weakening royal military power. Thus the internal balance of power moved away from the king to the *yangban* class.

As the *yangban* increased in number through each generation, so the competition for official posts increased. Rivalry and ambition led to a number of feuds and purges within the official class, as powerful *yangban* sought to exclude their rivals from office. The *yangban* class was in any case divided between its loyalty to the Crown and to its respective clans. It was also difficult to institutionalize opposition under the Confucian ethic that emphasized authority. The net result of this *yangban* factionalism was that the monarchy was further weakened and that the creative energy of the early Yi kings ebbed away.

Historical analogies are not always apt. But in this particular respect, the Korean kings of this period were not as fortunate as the Tudor monarchs of England who reigned at approximately the same time. These monarchs were able to establish their authority and also a centralized monarchy at the expense of the traditional landed aristocracy.

Eventually, however, a semblance of stability was restored to Korea during the early sixteenth-century reign of King Chungjong (1506–44). But for the remainder of the Yi dynasty, the Crown was, on the whole, at a disadvantage in relation to the reasserted power of the *yangban*.

Following Chungjong's reign, there was a revival of *yangban* factionalism. But within a generation, the internal problems of the Korean kings were relegated to a secondary place as relations with Japan came to the fore. Events within that neighboring island empire at the end of the sixteenth century were now to have profound results for Korea.

Hideyoshi's Invasion

During the fourteenth and fifteenth centuries, south and west Korea were plagued by Japanese pirates on Kyushu and the Tsushima islands in the Korea Strait. The founder of the Yi dynasty, King Taejo, had distinguished himself as a young man in operations against these pirates. Successive Korean kings had thus sent envoys to the Shogun's court at Kyoto in Japan with the objective of controlling these marauders. As the emperor was but a cipher, it was the Ashikaga Shogunate that ruled Japan.

Progress was made in controlling the piracy. During the early fifteenth century, there was a regular exchange of missions between Korea and the Shogunate. Some trade also developed between the two countries, which was largely controlled, by the *Daimyo* (lord) of Tsushima. A commercial treaty between Korea and the *Daimyo* in 1439 regularized this trade, and three south-eastern Korean ports, later reduced to one at Pusan, were opened to commerce.

Despite these trading activities, the political arena in Japan during the fifteenth and sixteenth centuries was characterized by almost perpetual civil war, in which rival *Daimyo* increasingly wrested authority from the Shogunate. But in 1573 there was a change in this pattern that soon affected Korea. A great Japanese warrior, Oda Nobunaga, overthrew the Ashikaga Shogunate and began to impose his rule on the country. Although Nobunaga was assassinated in 1582, one of his followers, Toyotomi Hideyoshi, now succeeded in unifying Japan and was given the title of dictator.

Hideyoshi, although physically a near-dwarf, was a great military leader and he now decided on the conquest of China. When the Koreans rejected Hideyoshi's demand for transit rights in this ambitious plan, a Japanese army of 150,000 men invaded Korea in the spring of 1592. Within three weeks of landing at Pusan, the Japanese had taken Seoul. By July, Pyongyang had fallen. A significant factor in these successes was the use of muskets by the Japanese. These they had copied from the Portuguese who had landed in Japan in 1542.

In response to a Korean request, large Ming Chinese forces now entered Korea across the Yalu, and forced the Japanese back to the vicinity of Seoul. Korean guerrillas harried the Japanese; and, under Admiral Yi Sun-sin, Korean ironclad warships— named "turtle-ships" after their armored decks—intercepted Japanese supply vessels in the Korea Strait. Further Japanese losses from disease were considerable. But the Chinese also suffered heavy losses, and many thousands of Koreans died in the chaos of war.

An armistice was agreed upon in 1593. But the Japanese, following further reverses, now only occupied a toehold of Korean territory in the south. The peace negotiations dragged on; and in 1597, Hideyoshi launched another full-scale invasion of Korea. But this time, the invaders only succeeded in occupying the southern Korean province of Kyongsang and part of Cholla. Admiral Yi won a decisive action over the Japanese fleet, but was killed in action. Only after Hideyoshi's death in 1598 did the Japanese withdraw from Korea.

Hideyoshi's invasion had profound consequences for the three countries involved. Tokugawa Ieyasu, Hideyoshi's successor, was able to become the recognized dictator of Japan, and later Shogun. He was the founder of the Tokugawa Shogunate that would rule until 1868. For Ming China, the years of fighting in Korea with its unprecedented cost were soon to lead to the collapse of the dynasty when faced with the militant challenge of the Manchus.

Admiral Yi Sun-sin and a "Turtle Ship" in 1592.

Korea was the most affected. The physical devastation was immense, and it is believed that land under cultivation fell by two-thirds. The southern Korean provinces were especially affected.

Temples, towns, and cultural treasures were all destroyed; while Korean potters, together with metal printing type and other artifacts were taken back to Japan. Resentment over the invasion naturally remained. But a treaty was signed with the Shogunate in 1609 that permitted limited trade between the two countries through Tsushima and Pusan.

The catastrophe of Hideyoshi's campaigns in Korea was compounded by the successive Manchu invasions of the country forty years later. Korea then withdrew from virtually all foreign contacts for over two hundred years, so acquiring the name of the "Hermit Kingdom." It is to this prolonged episode in Korean history that we must now turn.

CHAPTER 4

THE TIME OF ISOLATION

Within barely a generation of Hideyoshi's invasion, Korea was to suffer further foreign incursion, but this time from north of the Yalu. The Ming dynasty in China had been critically weakened by its efforts in repelling the Japanese from Korea; the Chinese rulers now faced the threat of the revived Jurched tribes of Manchuria—a people subsequently known to history as the Manchus.

The Manchus hoped to conquer China and to set up their own dynasty in much the same way as the Mongols had done. Moreover, like the Mongols, the Manchus were clearly aware of the potential flanking threat from a Korea loyal to the old Chinese dynasty.

The Manchu Invasions of Korea

It soon became apparent that the decline of the Ming was terminal. Taking advantage of their early military successes against the Ming and also of dissension within the Korean royal family, a Manchu army crossed the Yalu in 1627 and seized Pyongyang. The invaders then moved south to Seoul. King Injo (1623–49) and his family fled to the traditional royal retreat of Kanghwa Island in the Han estuary. But prolonged struggle was not possible, and peace negotiations were soon begun. The Koreans agreed to pay tribute to the Manchus, and also, in rather vague terms, to give homage.

The issue was finally decided during 1636–37, after the Manchus had won further victories over the Ming. By now the Manchus had proclaimed themselves the Ching dynasty of China, and their envoys demanded that Korea should formally become their vassal. King Injo refused and consequently another Manchu host invaded Korea. Like the Mongols four centuries previously, the invaders advanced through the central Korean mountains and southwards along the Uijongbu corridor that lies immediately north of Seoul.

This time King Injo and his family were unable to escape their fate. Although the king initially took up residence on Kanghwa Island, this royal sanctuary soon fell to the invaders. The king was then forced to renounce all allegiance to the Ming, and to make homage to the Manchu Ching dynasty. The Crown Prince of Korea, Prince Sohyon, was held by the Manchus as a hostage. Korea was also forced to assist the Manchus in their final military campaigns against the Ming regime, which was at last toppled in 1644. From Peking, the Manchus now ruled China as the Ching, a dynasty that was to survive until 1911.

These events, following the earlier Japanese invasions, were traumatic for Korea. The country was now to enjoy over two centuries of peace, but the fear of foreign countries was so great that foreign travel and foreign visitors were banned. It was these developments that gave Korea its name of the "Hermit Kingdom."

Foreign trade was also restricted and officially confined to China and Japan. Envoys and annual tribute were sent to the Imperial Court at Peking through the Korean town of Uiju on the

Yalu, and then through Mukden in southern Manchuria to Shanhaikuan, where the Great Wall of China meets the sea. The demands of the Ching were not heavy, and the tribute ritual continued well into the nineteenth century.

Trade with Japan was allowed on a restricted basis through Tsushima Island and Pusan. Occasionally, Korean envoys were sent to the court of the Shogun at Edo (later Tokyo). Following the virtual elimination of Christianity in early seventeenth-century Japan, that country was closed to foreigners on pain of death in 1638. Apart from the limited trade with Korea, the only external contact allowed by the Tokugawa Shogunate was a small Dutch trading post on the island of Deshima in Nagasaki harbor.

But Korea was even more effectively isolated than Japan. Korea relied on Peking for its foreign relations; and as an independent country within the Confucian system, it insisted that even the Sino-Korean border along the Yalu was kept tightly closed.

The result of this effective self-imposed seclusion—one underlined by geographical isolation—was that Korea was the last of the Confucian states of East Asia to be opened to Western contact. The full implications of this policy of national isolation only became apparent in the later nineteenth century. By then it was no longer possible to insulate even the Hermit Kingdom from the outside world.

The Hermit Kingdom

Korea's time of isolation from the seventeenth to the later nineteenth centuries was characterized on the whole by political and social stagnation; but, paradoxically, the tradition of artistic vitality dating from the early Yi period was maintained.

One of the leading Western authorities on East Asia, John K. Fairbank, has suggested that the picture of political stagnation may have been due in part to the fact that so much had been borrowed from China. But Fairbank also writes that Korea remained distinctly different from China "in historical experiences, social structure, and worldly situation. But like the Manchus when they ruled the Middle Kingdom, the Korean ruling class felt themselves to be conservators of a great tradition, not innovators."

Fairbank goes on to write that the hereditary and nonproductive *yangban* class used Chinese attitudes to support a monopoly of public life narrower than that of the gentry class in China. They clung to the letter of Confucianism, tolerated no deviation from orthodoxy, maintained private Confucian academies (*sowon*), and controlled the examination system. They also controlled and restricted trade, mining, and technical innovation.

The Japanese and Manchu invasions were partly responsible for this ascendancy of the *yangban*. The early Yi kings, as we have seen, had attempted to rule the country directly, and dispensed with the executive powers of the State Council, relegating this body to an advisory role. However, during the Japanese invasions and after, the Korean Army's Frontier Defense Command had increasingly emerged as a de facto executive State Council, combining both high military and civil officials. In effect, this new council administered the government for the king, so reverting to the situation that had existed in late Koryo times.

Depiction of the Yangban at Leisure by Sin Yunbok (b. 1758)

Following the Manchu invasions, this Council (now called the *Pibyonsa*) consolidated its powers and emerged as a permanent, institutionalized element of Yi government that was to survive into the nineteenth century. The accumulation of power by the early Yi monarchs was thus quite clearly reversed. In the absence of a strong monarchy, the *yangban* class was able to continue to reassert its power and privileges.

The decades following the Manchu invasions of Korea thus witnessed a new level of bureaucratic factionalism within the government. A series of feuds between "Southerners" and "Westerners" culminated in the triumph of the latter faction at the end of the seventeenth century. This victorious faction of "Westerners" then divided into the Noron (or elder group) and the Soron (younger group). By the early eighteenth century, the Noron were in the ascendant, excluding all other factions from power. Yet there were usually no serious policy differences at the center of this factionalism.

As a result of this internecine feuding, large numbers of *yangban* who found themselves excluded from office diverted their energies into expanding their country estates. The Confucian examination system for government personnel became increasingly irrelevant as the dominant faction within the court manipulated the results.

Under the rule of King Yongjo (1724–76) and King Chongjo (1776–1800), two successive monarchs attempted to end this bureaucratic rivalry by giving government posts to both the Noron and the Soron factions. But in a wider context, this factionalism indicated the collapse of the Confucian idealism that provided much of the inspiration of the early Yi kings.

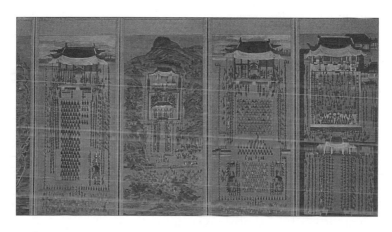

An Official Court Painting of King Chongjo.

According to the Korean historian Woo-keun Han, "although factionalism was for a time eliminated, power continued to depend upon wealth and position rather than talent, and the Confucian concepts that had contributed so much to Yi dynasty government and society no longer had any real influence on the actual practice of government."

But there were some positive developments in economic life during Korea's time of isolation. In the aftermath of the Manchu invasions, the tax system was partly rationalized in the interests of uniformity. Yet the overall tax burden demanded by the workings of the top-heavy royal administration in Seoul remained high. On the other hand, agricultural improvements meant that two-crop farming with barley and rice became common, at least in southern Korea. These improvements, combined with new irrigation techniques, led to a gradual increase of population. Thus the total population of Korea is believed to have grown from over two million in 1657 to over seven million in 1753.

There was a steady growth in the size of Seoul. This enlargement was partly due to the slow development of a mercantile economy that stemmed from the increase in national population and wealth. Despite the formal Confucian disapproval of commercial activity, displaced *yangban* increasingly entered business life in Seoul. Another development that pointed the way towards a less rigidly stratified society was the government's sale of some official posts to raise cash for the exchequer. Rich peasants also found themselves able to buy *yangban* estate titles as social mobility gradually increased.

Gradually, too, serfs and slaves won their freedom. In the aftermath of the Japanese and Manchu invasions that had left a devastated countryside, there was a labor shortage. Both an impoverished government and *yangban* class found it was cheaper to let slaves become tenants rather than to keep them. This process was underlined in 1801, when the registers of serfs or bondmen were destroyed by the government to assist the process of emancipation. As traditional Confucian society declined, so wealth rather than family became the indicator of status.

In contrast to this slow decay of Confucian society during the time of isolation, the period was one of continuing cultural achievement. During the eighteenth century, the Korean law codes were revised, and there were significant developments in studies affecting Korean history and geography. A new national consciousness began to form. Another significant development was the growth of the Sirhak (Practical Learning) movement amongst the intelligentsia. As its name implies, the movement demanded a practical approach to administration, rather than concentration on the tenets of Confucianism and on Chinese classical literature. This movement flourished in the eighteenth century.

In the visual arts, there were continuing achievements in calligraphy and especially in genre painting, with artists increasingly inspired by scenes drawn from everyday Korean life.

Thus Chang Son (d.1759), an especially innovative painter, depicted the Korean landscape in a variety of scenes; while Kim Hong-do (b.1740) painted scenes from the daily life of the common people. Another famous artist of this period, Sin Yunbok, painted romantic love scenes of men and women in striking colors and with decisive brushwork. While Chinese forms were still influential, the inspiration of these artists was specifically Korean.

"Clearing after the Rain on Inwang Mountain" by Chang Son.

"Mundong," or "A Dancing Boy" by Kim Hong-do.

"Lovers Under the Moon" by Sin Yunbok.

The Coming of the West

In the seventeenth and eighteenth centuries, European influence grew slowly but steadily in the Far East. In China and even in Japan, there was a growing awareness of Western scientific and technical knowledge amongst the elite.

But Korea was several hundred miles to the north of the Western trade routes, which extended from the Indian Ocean to southern China at Canton and to the Dutch trading post at Nagasaki in Japan. In any case, as we have noted, it was specifically forbidden for Koreans to have contact with other nations. Moreover the Confucian governing class in Korea believed that nothing could be learnt from any other foreign country but China.

During the seventeenth century, however, Chinese translations of Western books on science and religion began to enter Korea from the small Jesuit mission in Peking, which had been founded originally by the famous missionary Matteo Ricci (d.1610). These books were brought back to Seoul by Korean envoys to the Chinese Imperial Court. "Western Learning" (*Sohak*) made no appreciable impression on the Korean elite. But during the eighteenth century, the influence of Roman Catholic Christianity began to spread gradually among the people of western and southern Korea.

By the end of the century, many of the inhabitants of Hwanghae Province in northwestern Korea were reported to be sympathetic to Catholicism. The faith was also apparently popular in the southern provinces of Chungchong and Cholla. As Catholic influence began to spread amongst the *yangban* classes, the government now took counter-measures. The new religion was banned in 1795, and the import of Catholic books from China forbidden.

No ordained Christian minister had entered Korea until 1795, when the Chinese Catholic priest Chou Wen-mu crossed the Yalu. Prior to about this time, Catholicism had not been actively persecuted. But with the accession of boy-king Sunjo in 1800, there came a change of policy by the court's new advisers. Catholicism was now regarded as a subversive cult. The first large-scale persecution of Catholic adherents in 1801 cost the life of the priest Chou Wen-mu.

Catholicism was also regarded as a foreign creed that threatened the state, for about this time an appeal by a Korean Catholic for French naval assistance was intercepted by the authorities. The faith was soon driven underground, but continued to flourish, as so often in the past, despite persecution. French priests were sent to Korea from China; and in 1831, Korea was detached from the Catholic bishopric of Peking and made a see in its own right. A renewed wave of persecution soon followed in 1839, when three French priests were executed.

By 1850 there were about 11,000 Catholics in Korea, and by 1865 this number had doubled. A central element in this prolonged persecution, which lasted until 1873, was the official belief that Catholicism was associated with the foreign intervention that had cost Korea so much in the past. This concern was underlined by contemporary events that now ripped apart the old Confucian order in East Asia. Essentially these developments, which were to affect Korea profoundly, were caused by the inevitable collision between the dynamic, mercantile Western powers and the closed societies of China, Japan, and Korea.

Choldusan Cathedral, built at the site where Catholic believers were persecuted in the 19ᵗʰ Century.

By the treaty of Nanking (29 August 1842) that ended the Opium War the British were awarded Hong Kong and the opening of five Chinese "treaty ports" to British trade and residence. A supplementary treaty in 1843 put British subjects in the treaty ports under consular protection, so giving them extraterritorial status—a provision that was developed in all subsequent Sino-Western treaties. For the Celestial Empire, this was a humiliating end to the Opium War that was to cast a long shadow over subsequent events in the Far East.

In 1844 Chinese treaties with America and France consolidated the initial Western penetration of China. These and subsequent treaties that China, Japan, and finally Korea made with the Western powers all incorporated a "most-favored-nation" clause that automatically gave to each Western signatory those privileges that might later be given to another power. So a whole system of "treaty law" came into existence in the Far East that underwrote Western commercial penetration.

After China, Japan was the next ancient state of the East Asia to be "opened." Ever since the turn of the century, British and American clippers had sailed close to its forbidden shores, but all attempts to initiate trading relations had failed. At last, in 1853, Commodore Matthew Perry entered Tokyo Bay with a small but very powerful naval task force. The shogunate was unable to resist and the ensuing Treaty of Kanagawa (31 March 1854) opened two Japanese ports to American trade. The Japanese also conceded a most-favored-nation clause.

A parallel treaty was signed in 1854 between the Japanese and the British, and the following year with the Russian Empire. Another treaty was later signed with the Dutch. In 1858 these four powers, together with France, signed a further round of commercial treaties with Japan, "The Treaties with the Five Powers." After more than two centuries of isolation Japan had been opened to the West.

In the wake of the Japanese treaties, Western penetration of China was now carried considerably further by Anglo-French operations in China during 1856–60. After several years of tension, Anglo-French military action in north China had initially ended in treaties signed between the two powers and China at Tienstin in June 1858. The concessions won by Britain and France were also awarded in similar treaties signed by American and Russian envoys. These treaties also provided for permanent Western missions in Peking, which went far towards ending China's ancient assumption of superiority over the Western barbarians.

The Chinese were dilatory in implementing the 1858 treaties. The issue was now put beyond doubt when formidable Anglo-French forces returned to north China in 1860 and fought their way into Peking in October of that year. The Emperor fled beyond the Great Wall and his brother, Prince Kung, signed new treaties with new concessions to the powers, which in effect opened the whole of China to international trade. America and Russia shared these concessions under the "most-favored-nation" clause.

Of particular significance for Korea were the quite separate Sino-Russian accords of 1858 and 1860 that began the large-scale dismemberment of China. By the Treaty of Aigun (May 1858), the Chinese conveyed to the Russian Empire the extensive Manchu lands north of the Amur River bordering the Pacific. The large Manchu Maritime Province between the Ussuri River and the Pacific, with its great strategic potential, was placed under joint Sino-Russian administration.

Two years later, the Sino-Russian Treaty of Peking (November 1860) gave the entire Maritime Province to the Russian Empire, which now had an eleven-mile border with Korea along the estuary of the Tumen River. A hundred miles to the east, the Russians had already founded the port of Vladivostok ("Rule of the East") in the summer of 1860.

These historic events, and the increasing activity of Western vessels off the Korean coast, now led to international speculation as to which Western nation would be the first to open the last of the closed societies of East Asia. But the initial Korean reaction to the opening of China and Japan was to draw closer than ever into its isolation.

Revolt and Limited Reform

Like China and Japan in the 1850s and 1860s, the old order in Korea faced an internal as well as an external challenge. In China the Taiping rebellion—a highly nationalist reform movement that was part Chinese and part Christian in its intellectual origins—took over large parts of South China between 1850 and 1864, when it was finally defeated by the Imperial government. In Japan, as we shall see below, a group of southwestern clans with Imperial connivance, overthrew the Tokugawa Shogunate following a short civil war during 1867–68.

Internal developments in Korea were distinct from both China and Japan. During the early 1860s, a new religious cult made its appearance that provided the inspiration for serious peasant revolt in southern Korea during 1862–64. The cult was not only a protest against poverty and bad government, but as its name of *Tonghak* ("Eastern Learning") indicated, it was a reaction against the gradual spread in Korea of "Western Learning," now increasingly identified with Catholicism. The founder of the *Tonghak* creed was Ch'oe Che-u (b. 1824), the son of an impoverished *yangban* family from Kyongsang province in southeast Korea.

It appears that Choe was partly inspired by the Taiping rebellion in China, and also by news of the concessions forced from the Emperor by the Anglo-French operations of 1856–60. Choe claimed to have received a divine message during 1860 to create a new religion that would restore the East to primacy over the West.

The roots of this utopian cult lay in a mixture of Buddhism, Confucianism, and Taoism with a distinct element of shamanism—the indigenous Korean animistic religion still rooted in the peasant classes, which of course pre-dated Buddhism and Confucianism. Understandably the *Tonghak* creed had a special appeal for peasants and tenant farmers at the lower end of the social scale; agricultural discontent in Korea was endemic following a series of natural disasters in the earlier part of the century.

The *Tonghak* movement claimed to be strongly anti-Catholic. But the authorities distrusted the clearly subversive elements in the creed; Choe was captured, tried, and executed in 1864 at Taegu, in his native province. But he left behind him many followers and the movement continued to spread, underground, throughout Korea. In a wider context, the *Tonghak* movement, like the Catholicism it opposed, indicated the continuing disintegration

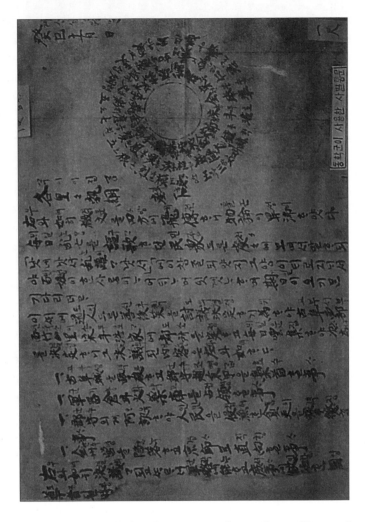

Document that Tonghak Believers passed as a Secret Means of Communication.

of traditional Korean Confucian society with its emphasis on a changeless hierarchy.

But the challenge posed by the *Tonghak* movement was met by determined counter-measures on the part of the authorities. With the death of King Ch'olchong in 1864, the boy-king Yi Myong-bok came to the throne. King Kojong, to give him his posthumous title, was to rule until 1907, and was the penultimate Yi monarch. But his youth meant that his father, Yi Ha-ung (d. 1898) was appointed Regent. He was to be known by his title of Taewongun ("Lord of the Great Court").

The Taewongun was one of the most forceful characters in later Korean history, and he was to rule in the name of his son for the next decade until 1873. He was determined to meet both the internal challenge of the *Tonghak* and the Catholics and the external threat of the Western powers by a strictly applied policy of conservative reform. This policy aimed at restoring traditional Confucian society. There was thus a distinct element of idealism in the Taewongun's approach.

In accordance with his policy, the Taewongun took measures to strengthen the royal powers. He also tried to eliminate *yangban* factionalism, the curse of Korean politics, by closing most of the private Confucian academies—the *sowon*, to which we have referred. The Taewongun also embarked on a process of legal reform as part of his policy of improving the central administration.

Another aspect of the Taewongun's reforms was the building of a small modern army, and the creation of new coastal defenses for use against the barbarians. The corollary of this policy was, of course, increased taxation. There was also renewed, severe, and prolonged persecution of Catholics.

Initially, the Taewongun's exclusionist policy seemed to work. In 1866 the American trading vessel, *General Sherman*, tried to enter the Taedong estuary on the northwestern Korean coast that leads to Pyongyang. The ship was sunk with all hands. That same year, the execution of French Catholic priests brought a small French fleet to the mouth of the Han River. French troops landed on Kanghwa Island and even occupied Kanghwa town as a reprisal, but these intruders were beaten off.

During 1867–68, American warships off the Korean west coast tried to discover the fate of the *General Sherman*, but without avail. In 1871, the American Minister to China was sent to the Han estuary with five warships. American troops then occupied the Kanghwa Island forts, not without resistance and a number of casualties on both sides. But the Koreans refused to negotiate, and the American expedition withdrew. The Taewongun continued, meanwhile, with the anti-Catholic persecutions, and evidently believed that these limited successes against the Western barbarians justified his policy of continuing isolation.

This was a mistaken view, for the Western powers in the Far East were preoccupied with developing their newly-won concessions in China and Japan. Korea was secondary to these interests. A more significant miscalculation was to ignore developments in Japan after the successful revolt against the Shogunate during 1867–68.

In early 1868, the samurai and nobles now in the ascendant formally "restored" the powers of the young Emperor Mutsuhito. He took the name Meiji ("Enlightened Rule") for his reign and moved the capital from Kyoto to Edo, which was now renamed Tokyo ("Eastern Capital"). Under the policies of the

US Marines land on Kangwha Island in 1871.

Meiji restoration, Japan embarked on a systematic and far-reaching modernization of its government, economic structure, and armed forces, drawing on the best-available Western models. Meiji institutions generally were to show a great ability to adapt.

This policy meant, of course, that Japan was now increasingly able to resist Western political and economic pressure. It seems likely that only a parallel policy could have saved Korea from subsequent foreign intervention.

As early as 1870, the new Meiji administration in Tokyo attempted to open diplomatic relations with Korea. But this attempt was ignored by the Taewongun who characteristically disliked the passing of the Shogunate. In 1872 a Japanese delegation appeared at Tongnae, near Pusan, but was refused official permission to proceed to Seoul. Evidently the Taewongun, and the Yi bureaucracy, believed the Japanese could be denied admission to Korea.

The Taewongun was removed from office in 1873, and King Kojong took over his full powers. But the former regent's exclusionist policies remained. Thus another Japanese delegation to Tongnae in 1875 was rebuffed. But Meiji Japan, slowly growing in self-confidence, was determined to enter Korea. The Hermit Kingdom's long period of self-imposed isolation was now at an end.

CHAPTER 5

THE OPENING OF KOREA

Following the Western example, the Japanese decided in late 1875 to back their demands for trading relations with Korea by a show of force. A Japanese battleship and another warship sailed up the Korean east coast from Pusan to the vicinity of the northern harbor of Wonsan, and then returned to the west coast. The Japanese warships then anchored off the port of Inchon, which lies on the Yellow Sea about eighteen miles west of Seoul, and which was then still known by its old name of Chemulpo.

The Kanghwa Treaty

A small Japanese contingent then landed on nearby Kanghwa Island, the traditional refuge of the Korean court; there was a skirmish, and the Japanese withdrew. But the Japanese soon notified the Koreans that negotiations must now begin. After considerable hesitation by the Koreans, talks then started on Kanghwa Island. Eventually on 26 February 1876, a commercial treaty based on Western models was signed. The accord opened three Korean ports for Japanese trade: Pusan, Wonsan, and Inchon. The treaty also provided for an exchange of diplomatic missions and gave extraterritorial rights to the Japanese in Korea. Japanese diplomats were allowed freedom of travel.

The Kanghwa Treaty also stipulated that Korea "being an independent state enjoys the same sovereign rights as Japan." This statement meant, of course, that Japan was attempting to remove Korea from its traditional tributary relationship with China as a means of facilitating Japanese freedom of action, both commercially and politically. But the Chinese, on the other hand, were determined to retain their interests and their influence within Korea. An important element in this contest, inherent in the opening of Korea, was the rivalry between the traditionalists (or conservatives) and the modernizers (or reformers) in Korea as the country now began to react to the foreign influences so long proscribed.

Traditionalists and Modernizers

Although Japanese trade now began to enter Korea through Pusan, there was still strong opposition to the Kanghwa Treaty from the traditionalist elite within Korea. Wonsan was only opened to Japan in 1880 and Inchon in 1883. Meanwhile, the Chinese advised the Korean court to embark on treaty relations with the Western powers as a means of countering Japanese and Russian pressure. The Chinese also hoped to forestall external pressure on Korea by sponsoring a limited amount of modernization, parallel to that being attempted in China itself.

In line with the Chinese policy of playing off the foreign barbarians against each other, Korea signed a treaty of "friendship, commerce and navigation" with the United States on 22 May 1882. A similar treaty was signed with Great Britain the following month. The customs terms were not considered favorable enough by the British Foreign Office, however, and a revised Korean-British treaty was later signed on 26 November 1883. A Korean Treaty with the German Empire was signed the same day. Other treaties followed with Italy and Russia (1884) and France (1886).

These treaties recognized Korean independence. But the contradiction remained between Korea's tributary role in the Confucian system and the precise sovereign status accorded the country under Western international law. Yet most Western countries recognized that there was something special in the Chinese-Korean relationship. Subsequent to the American-Korean treaty, for example, the United States agreed to accept a letter from the Korean king stating that the treaty had been made with Chinese consent; and initially, most of the first Western legations in Seoul were placed under the jurisdiction of the parent missions in Peking.

Western diplomats, traders, missionaries, writers and other visitors now began to enter Korea in increasing numbers. The concept of modernizing reform (*Kaewha*) began to gain adherents within Korea. Initially this concept meant a willingness to acquire Western knowledge and technology. Thus during the 1880s, the telegraph, electricity, and other Western inventions and services entered Korea. Newspapers were published, and modern postal services arrived. Western-type schools were established, and literacy increased.

Soon *Kaewha* also came to encompass the modification of Korean institutions to the new ways. During the early 1880s, the leading modernizers, who came to be known as the Independence Party, seemed to favor Japan as an example in view of that country's greater efficiency in promoting internal reform than

China. The reformers began to object to the increasing Chinese influence in Korea, and especially in the Korean Court.

China in the Ascendant

Despite the challenge posed by Japan and the Western powers, China was able to remain the predominant power in Korea from the early 1880s to 1894. There were several reasons why this was so. In general, Confucian intellectual influences and sympathy with the old order remained strong. Traditional Korean dislike of foreigners was another element. In particular, King Kojong's queen was a conservative influence who backed Chinese policies in general. She came from the powerful Min family and was, however, known as "Queen Min." The Korean court was thus, on the whole, against radical change and certainly not sympathetic to those modernizers who looked across the Korea Strait to Japan.

Events also played into Chinese hands. A brief but violent army revolt in Seoul in July 1882 precipitated the dispatch of a Chinese presence to Korea that was to last for over a decade. During this rebellion, which was motivated by anti-foreign nationalist sentiment and by concern over official corruption involving Queen Min's relatives, the Japanese legation in Seoul was attacked; high court officials were also killed. Queen Min was forced to flee the capital.

Both Chinese and Japanese forces were sent to Seoul to restore order, but the Chinese detachments were the bigger. In compensation, Japan was given new trading privileges. But China now began to actively supervise Korean political and economic affairs.

King Kojong with his Senior Ministers.

Chinese policy in Korea was overseen by an able statesman named Li Hung-chang; while the Chinese garrison in Seoul was commanded by an efficient, autocratic general, Yuan Shih-k'ai. A new Sino-Korean trading agreement, signed late in 1882, reaffirmed the traditional Chinese suzerainty over Korea. This traditional relationship gave the Chinese great latitude in their activities in Korea. But as we have seen, the relationship was not based on a treaty or legal agreement in the Western sense. Rather, it was based on a Confucian family understanding between China and Korea that reached back to the beginnings of the Korean kingdom.

The Korean court thus became (and remained) a focus of pro-Chinese traditionalism. Yet the very ascendancy of the Chinese faction spurred the modernizers to greater efforts. They were helped to a certain degree by the growing foreign missionary element in Korea. Contact with these foreigners widened the reformers' ambitions, and also introduced them to the latest Western ideas.

Kim Ok-kyun, the leader of the Independents, meanwhile visited Japan during late 1882. He soon came to believe that only the forcible removal of Queen Min and her faction would ensure the success of the Independents and their modernizing policies. Kim may also have believed that such action would correspond to the Meiji revolution of 1868 in Japan. At any rate, for their own reasons, the Japanese supported Kim in his plans.

During early December 1884, the Independents launched their coup d'etat. King Kojong was seized, a number of royal officials were killed, and a new modernizing government proclaimed. The coup was backed to the hilt by Japanese troops in

The Site of the December 1884 coup d'etat.

Seoul, clearly as a result of pre-arrangement. But the larger contingents of Chinese troops under General Yuan reacted swiftly and crushed the insurrection. Kim Ok-kyun and the Japanese Minister in Seoul barely escaped to a Japanese ship in Inchon.

Eventually, the differences between China and Japan were patched up, for the time being. Japanese and Chinese representatives, meeting at Tientsin in 1885, agreed to withdraw their military forces from Korea, and to inform each other before returning there. However General Yuan Shih-k'ai remained in Seoul as the grandly-styled "Supervisor for Foreign Affairs in Korea."

Some civil and military reforms were instituted under Chinese sponsorship and Chinese economic presence in Korea flourished at the expense of the Japanese. But decisive reforms and systematic modernization remained unlikely as long as the Korean court remained attached to the traditional Chinese connection.

Great Power Rivalries in Korea

Although the Chinese ascendancy in Seoul after the abortive coup of December 1884 seemed reassuring to the traditionalists, the long-term prospects for continuing Korean independence were not good.

The country's prolonged isolation and now the traditionalist resistance to reform weakened the possibility of effective resistance to outside pressure. The conflict between Westernizing reformers and the Confucian establishment in the 1880s recalled the self-destructive factionalism of earlier Korean history. Increasingly, these factions came to be allied to outside forces, a process that quite overtly threatened Korean independence.

During the 1880s, it also became clear that Korea was increasingly at the mercy of the great-power rivalries that were now coming to a climax in the Far East. To be sure, American and British diplomats and business interests were soon evident in Seoul after the signing of the commercial treaties in the early 1880s. But strategic rather than commercial interests were now to dictate the course of Korean history for the next two decades. Initially events pointed towards a showdown between China and Japan over Korea.

On paper, the Chinese position in Korea seemed strong. The traditional cultural links, geographical proximity, and a forceful representative in Seoul in the person of General Yuan Shih-k'ai all seemed to point towards renewed Chinese paramountcy for the foreseeable future.

Yet the Chinese position in Korea was weaker than it seemed. Japanese agreement with China over a mutual troop withdrawal in 1885 was based on a conscious decision of national policy in Tokyo to avoid a foreign war, pending the creation of a strong military establishment. German instructors were attached to the Japanese army, while British counterparts supervised the creation of a modern navy—soon to prove itself second to none in the Far East.

In essence the Japanese believed that the headlong modernizing process in their country gave them a growing military capability that would soon offset China's traditional advantages in any conflict over Korea. Japanese diplomatic and commercial pressure continued unabated in Korea and Korean modernizers still looked to Japan.

Japan's growing strength was only part of the pattern of international rivalry that now increasingly centered on Korea. During the negotiations of the Russian-Korean commercial treaty in 1884, St. Petersburg had indicated that it was willing to modernize the Korean Army in exchange for a warm-water port in southern Korea near Pusan. The Russians were also interested in obtaining facilities at Wonsan, on the northeastern coast. Underlying the Russian drive for a warm-water port in Korea was the fact that Vladivostok was ice-bound for three or four months annually.

As a precaution against Russian naval activity in Korean waters, the Royal Navy occupied Komun Island, off the Korean south coast, in 1885. This was a strategically placed anchorage, known as Port Hamilton, which gave control of the Korea Strait. Eventually, the British withdrew their ships during 1887, following Russian assurances that occupation of Korea territory was not considered. A tombstone recording the death of two British sailors in 1886 remains on Komun Island to commemorate this fleeting episode.

The failure of the Russians to gain any significant advantage in Korea following their commercial treaty in 1884 indicated their general strategic weakness in the Far East. The enormous distances that separated Vladivostok from European Russia, combined with inferior Russian naval resources in relation to the Western powers, precluded the effective projection of St. Petersburg's ambitions in the region.

During 1886 the Czar Alexander III decided to redress the strategic balance by the construction of a 6,000-mile Trans-Siberian railway from Moscow to Vladivostok. The railway, when completed, would enable the Russian Empire to send large numbers of troops to the Far East. St. Petersburg would thus be able to pursue more effectively its policies in China and Korea, and to offset Japan's growing strength. Construction of the railway began from both ends in 1891. It was hoped to complete the immense project in little over a decade. Meanwhile, the primary rivalry over Korea remained that between China and Japan.

Sino-Japanese War, 1894–95

Domestic events within Korea now brought this simmering Sino-Japanese rivalry to a head. Although the founder of the *Tonghak* creed, Ch'oe Che-u, had been executed in 1864, his doctrines lived on. His followers continued to meet in the hills of southern Korea. As a result of continuing rural poverty and deprivation, the *Tonghak* leaders presented a petition to King Kojong in early 1893. The petition was rejected and the *Tonghak* followers were told to return home. The road to peaceful reform seemed closed.

Endemic rural discontent now broke into open rebellion, and by the spring of 1894 the three southern provinces of Cholla, Kyongsang, and Chungchong were affected. At the end of May 1894 Chonju, the provincial capital of Cholla, fell to the insurgents. The *Tonghak* now put forward demands for sweeping reforms.

Although the Korean military was able to recapture Chonju, King Kojong asked for Chinese assistance to crush the rebellion in the south. This act was done against advice, yet it was a traditional request for a Korean monarch who looked instinctively to Peking in times of national danger. But this time, a request for Chinese assistance was to lead to a chain of events that would end forever Korea's formal dependency on China.

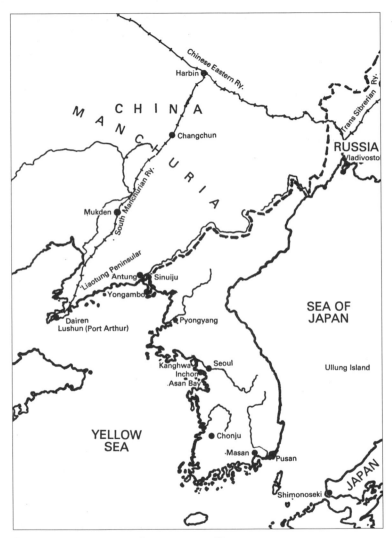

Sino-Japanese Russo-Japanese conflicts.

Following this Korean request to Peking, Chinese warships and troop transports were sent to Inchon and to Asan Bay on the Korean west coast. The Japanese also sent troops to Inchon, ostensibly to protect their legation in Seoul. China responded with further troop reinforcements, and so did the Japanese, who did not of course recognize China's claim to suzerainty over Korea. Japan also claimed that it had the right to send its troops to Korea under the Sino-Japanese accord reached at Tienstin in 1885.

Initially both sides seemed to act pre-emptively in fear of the other. But as the stakes were raised, the Chinese apparently came to believe that the military advantage was theirs. The Chinese were further disposed to act following the Japanese sinking of the British steamer *Kowshing*, which was ferrying Chinese troops to Korea. The outcome of the *Tonghak* rebellion was now relegated to second place, as the issue became one of which power would win this historic confrontation over Korea.

The Japanese proposed that the Korean government institute fundamental reforms under Sino-Japanese supervision—a course of action that would certainly terminate Chinese influence in Korea. When the Koreans refused to consider this plan, the Japanese military occupied the Kyongbok Palace in Seoul on 23 July 1894, so capturing King Kojong and his court. Queen Min, the symbol of the court's pro-Chinese policy, was forced out of Seoul and so was the Chinese General, Yuan Shih-k'ai.

Japan now acted with great speed and decision. On 25 July, without declaring hostilities, the Japanese navy attacked Chinese ships at Asan Bay. Japanese troops marched south from Seoul to defeat the Chinese at Kongju. China and Japan then declared war on 1 August. The Japanese also forced the Korean court to declare war against China. King Kongjo, in Japanese hands, signed a number of accords that, in effect, gave Japan a free military hand in Korea for the duration of hostilities.

To the south of Seoul, Japanese and royal Korean units now quickly crushed the *Tonghak* rebels. But the Japanese main force in Korea struck north to Pyongyang, defeating the Chinese. The Japanese then swept on northwards, crossed the Yalu, and advanced into southern Manchuria, taking the Liaotung Peninsula, and with it the modern fortress of Port Arthur (Lushun), which fell in November 1894.

The key to these Japanese victories—which changed the world's perception of Japan—lay in Japan's naval supremacy, for Chinese resupply in Korea was by sea. Overall, the Chinese had about 65 warships to Japan's 32, so that the advantage seemed to lie with the Ching fleet. When the opposing fleets met off the mouth of the Yalu in the Yellow Sea on 17 September 1894 each side deployed 12 ships. But the Japanese had faster vessels, better gunnery, and more effective tactics. Four Chinese warships were sunk, while the Japanese suffered no losses. Thereafter Japan dominated Korean waters.

Following these Japanese successes, the Chinese Empire had no alternative but to sue for peace. China then made many concessions in the Treaty of Shimonoseki, signed in that Japanese port on 17 April 1895.

The Chinese were forced to give Formosa and the Pescadores to Japan and also ceded the Liaotung Peninsula and Port Arthur. This naval base, named after the French military engineer, William Arthur, who had fortified the Chinese seaport of Lushun in the early 1880s, dominated the Yellow Sea. The Chinese also agreed to negotiate a new commercial treaty with Japan. In the event, this trading accord gave the Japanese all the Western privileges in China, and yet further concessions.

As for Korea, the Chinese finally relinquished all their historic tributary claims, for the Treaty of Shimonoseki stipulated that "China recognizes definitively the full and complete independence and autonomy of Korea, and in consequence the payment of tribute and the performance of ceremonies and formalities by Korea to China, in derogation of such independence and autonomy, shall wholly cease for the future."

Korea was now formally independent, a sovereign state in the full meaning of the term as understood in Western international law. But this new status was an ambivalent achievement, for the Treaty of Shimonoseki only ushered in a new and even more bitter struggle between Japan and Russia for supremacy in Korea.

CHAPTER 6

JAPAN AND RUSSIA IN KOREA, 1895–1910

Although Japan's great victory over China brought it general Western recognition as one of the leading nations in the Far East, it also aroused conflicting attitudes amongst the powers. In the United States and Great Britain, there had been admiration for Japanese military efficiency (and pride in the way that Japan had learnt from the West). The Czarist government, however, was concerned that the overwhelming Japanese success might result in a check to Russia's own ambitions in Manchuria and Korea. Russian diplomacy was extremely active in the Far East at this time; the continuing construction of the Trans-Siberian railway emphasized Russian interest in the region.

In line with this concern over Japan's victory and in the immediate aftermath of the Treaty of Shimonosehi in April 1895, St. Petersburg now organized a Russian-French-German diplomatic intervention. This de'marche forced Japan to abandon the Liaotung Peninsula and with it Port Arthur. As the Russians were apparently ready to back the "advice" of the "Triple Intervention" by military means, Japan had no alternative but to abandon the territory involved in exchange for a large additional indemnity from China. It was a necessary but humiliating retreat that was not forgotten in Tokyo.

Following the Triple Intervention, Korea quickly became the cockpit of Russo-Japanese rivalry in the Far East. Japan now discovered that despite the withdrawal of China from Korea and the emergence of a legally independent Korean state in the Western sense, it was confronted in Korea with a far more determined and powerful adversary than China. In addition, Japanese influence in Korean domestic politics was soon to suffer a serious reverse in favor of the Russians.

To be sure, in the immediate aftermath of the Japanese seizure of the Korean court in July 1894, the prospects for advancing Japanese influence seemed good. A new Korean Reform Council passed a number of fundamental reforms that were approved by the Japanese. A governmental structure with eight ministries, headed by a Prime Minister, was created. A new examination syllabus for state service was devised that superceded the old Confucian models. The local government system was re-cast.

The Korean court also tried to reform the chaotic Korean financial system by setting up a centralized Ministry of Finance to integrate the many local taxation systems that existed in the country. A new coinage was issued. The customary privileges of the *yangban* class were abolished, as were the traditional four classes of Korean society, to which we have already referred. There was a reorganization of the police, the judiciary, and the small Korean army. Concurrently, the Christian missionaries in Korea, especially the Protestants, continued to expand their educational programs. A new, self-conscious Korean nationalism began to emerge out of the old, traditional isolationism.

Queen Min Murdered

On paper, the infrastructure of a modern state began to appear in Korea. When the new cabinet took over at the end of 1894, a fourteen-point "Great Plan"—a summary of over two hundred reform measures—was promulgated. This de facto Constitution stressed that Korea was a fully independent state, that the royal court and the government were to be separate, and that reformed law codes were to be issued. During January 1895, King Kojong and his family went to Chongmyo, the Royal Ancestral Shrine of the Yi kings in Seoul, to announce the reforms to his ancestors.

The new reform program was formally completed by April 1895. But implementation was naturally difficult in view of the speed with which the program had been promulgated. The new measures also met resistance because they were associated with the Japanese. In the vanguard of the opposition to the reforms was Queen Min, the champion of the traditionalists.

Once again, external events began to affect developments within Korea. Following the "Triple Intervention" that had forced the Japanese to abandon Port Arthur, the Korean court now began to turn to the Russians, as in the past they had turned to the Chinese, to counteract Japanese influence. Queen Min was naturally active in these intrigues. Gradually, pro-Japanese ministers were eased out of the new administration by the influence of the court.

The Japanese in Seoul, through the person of their new Minister, Miura Goro, now overplayed their hand. It will be recalled that in July 1894, at the opening of the Sino-Japanese war, the Japanese had taken over the Korean court, forcing Queen Min out of Seoul. This time the Japanese evidently decided to eliminate Queen Min, the center of anti-Japanese opposition, for good.

On 8 October 1895, a party of Japanese agents and soldiers accompanied by disaffected Koreans from a military training unit, stormed the royal Kyongbok Palace and killed Queen Min. Her body was burnt in the Palace grounds. King Kojong was seized, and some royal officials were killed.

The Japanese evidently hoped to restore a government more sympathetic to their policies but had miscalculated. There was a storm of international protest, and the Japanese government distanced itself from the deed. Miura and some of his associates were later tried, but released due to "lack of evidence." There was mounting unrest throughout Korea during the winter of 1895–96, and eventually the Russian Minister arranged for over 200 armed Russian sailors to come to Seoul from a Russian warship anchored at Inchon. Ostensibly these men were extra guards for the Russian legation.

On 11 February 1896, through connivance with court officials, and protected by the Russians, King Kojong fled from the Kyongbok Palace to the Russian legation in Seoul. The pro-Japanese Korean premier was killed by a mob, and the Japanese were deterred from further action by the knowledge that an attack on the Russian legation could be construed as an act of war. A new pro-Russian government was formed.

The Japanese soon accepted the fait accompli and agreed with the Russian Minister in Seoul to jointly limit their forces in the Korean capital. It was also agreed that the king could live where he wished, and choose whatever ministers he wanted. Russian influence was now completely in the ascendant. An agreement between the Russian and Korean governments in May 1896 arranged for Russian military and financial advisers to be sent to Korea. Further Russian troops were to be sent, if necessary.

Japan remained in a strong economic position in Korea, and bided its time. For the present, however, King Kojong and Korean sovereignty were under Russian protection. The Japanese had suffered a serious political reverse.

The Independence Club

Although the physical security of the Korean court was improved by its transfer to the Russian legation in Seoul, its prestige suffered. A further source of weakness lay in the numerous foreign concessions that were increasingly handed out by the Korean government. These concessions granted rights for the development of minerals, timber, and other commodities. The Russians pressed for the concession of Choryong Island near Pusan, while the Japanese obtained extensive rights to build a railway from Pusan, through Seoul, to Uiju on the Yalu. American, British, and French interests were also involved in these concessions.

In these circumstances, there was a renewed growth of the modernizing reform movement, which now attracted increasing support. In particular, the movement began to crystallize around the person of So Chae-p'il, who had been one of the leaders of the abortive coup of December 1884.

So Chae-p'il had escaped to the United States, where he had acquired both American citizenship and a degree in medicine. He took the Western name of "Philip Jaisohn." In early 1896, Jaisohn returned to Korea and founded the Independence Club (*Tongnip*

Tognipmun Gate, built by the Independence Club in 1896.

Hyophoe), which was a reformist political grouping. He also founded a newspaper, *The Independent (Tongnip Shinmun)*, which was published three times weekly in English and in the indigenous Korean script, *Hangul*. Jaisohn considered the intensive promotion of *Hangul* an integral part of the reform movement.

The first issue of *The Independent*, published in Seoul on 7 April 1896, proclaimed that its platform was "Korea for the Koreans, clean politics, the cementing of foreign friendships . . ." *The Independent* also called for the speedy translation of foreign texts into Korean so that Korean youth might have access "to the great things of history, science, art and religion without having to acquire a foreign tongue. . ."

The Independent continued to promote Korean literacy, and also a variety of reform causes. It criticized corruption and mal-administration. The newspaper was written in a clear, forceful style, and its circulation soon rose from 300 to over 3,000. Mean-while, the Independence Club organized mass meetings and called for a continuing policy of government reform. There was a strong emphasis on popular education. One of the many sup-porters of the Independence Club was a young Korean patriot called Yi Sung-man, later known as Syngman Rhee (1875–1965), who after many vicissitudes in the cause of Korean nationalism would eventually become the first President of the Republic of Korea in 1948.

During 1897 the Independence movement became increas-ingly concerned with the great-power threat to Korea, and in particular with the number of foreign concessions that had been granted. Philip Jaisohn called for the king to leave the Russian legation. On 20 February 1897, King Kojong left

Russian protection and established his court in the Kyongun Royal Palace; his security was assured for this palace stood near the foreign legations in Seoul. After Kojong's eventual abdication in 1907, the Kyongun was renamed in his honor the Toksu Palace (The Palace of the Virtuous Longevity).

As part of the growing awakening in which the reform movement was playing such an important part, it was decided to change the king's title to Emperor. The word king meant, in Chinese, a ruler subordinate to the Chinese Emperor. The title of the Japanese Emperor made him semantically the equal of his counterpart in Peking. Accordingly King Kojong was crowned Emperor of Korea on 12 October 1897.

The new royal title had little practical effect on the number of important concessions still being awarded to the Russians. In the far north of Korea, the Russians were awarded valuable timber concessions along the Yalu. Further concessions were given to them on Ullung Island (Dagelet) in the Sea of Japan. During early 1898, a Russian bank appeared in Seoul, and it was rumored that this institution would henceforth supervise the operations of the Korean treasury.

There were vigorous protests over these developments, and the Russian bank was closed. Russian military advisers who had been sent to Korea in 1896 were also withdrawn. The Russians were unable to obtain the concession of Choryong Island, which would have given them control of Pusan harbor.

Originally, the Korean government had supported the new reform movement. But as the reformers increasingly criticized the vested interests of the conservative Korean court, the Independence Club became an embarrassment. First, Philip Jaisohn

Sokchojon Hall in Toksu Palace.

was forced to leave Korea. Then, after a series of street demonstrations and clashes later in 1898, the Independence Club was dissolved and some of its leaders arrested. Others fled from Korea. *The Independent* was closed down. The reform movement was suppressed.

The reformers had thus failed in many of their objectives. They were essentially an urban reform group, and had failed to develop a following in the countryside where rural discontent was unabated. But the memory of the Independence Club, and of *The Independent*, lived on to inspire later twentieth-century Korean nationalists.

Another important legacy of the Independence Club was the gradually increasing use of *Hangul*. Eventually, in 1907, the National Language Research Institute was established. Soon the exclusive use of Chinese in official documents was replaced by a mixture of selected Chinese characters and *Hangul*. Books and other publications began to use this new mixed system.

There was also continuing research on the Korean language, which scholars increasingly saw as the basis of the national spirit and the national tradition. Thus despite the Japanese annexation of Korea in 1910, a new Korean literary movement began to develop after this date.

Russo-Japanese War

During the late 1890s, the rivalry between Japan and Russia over Korea acquired a new momentum. Initially, both powers had made a half-hearted attempt at reconciliation. In June 1896, for example, both countries had agreed at St. Petersburg—during the prolonged coronation ceremonies of Czar Nicholas II—that if it became necessary for either to reinforce their troops in Korea the other country would be informed.

The Japanese had also suggested at this time, the partition of Korea into spheres of influence along the 38th Parallel, a demarcation line that would appear again in Korean history. But the Russian foreign minister, Alexei Lobanoff, declined the compromise. This refusal was only natural given the Russian interest in the warm-water anchorages of southern Korea—a zone that would fall to Japan under this proposed partition.

The Russians were indifferent to a comprehensive settlement with Japan over Korea because they calculated that the regional balance of power was moving in their favor. During the Czarist coronation period referred to above, Russia signed a secret alliance with China with far-reaching consequences. By this agreement, Russia was allowed to build a 1,000-mile long railway, across Manchuria from Lupin in Siberia towards Vladivostok. This railway, to be known as the Chinese Eastern Railway, provided a short cut for the main Trans-Siberian line, which necessarily swung north above the Amur River Manchurian frontier on its way to Vladivostok.

This initial Russian penetration of Manchuria was followed in March 1898 by the Russian lease of the Liaotung Peninsula, together with Port Arthur and the commercial harbor of Ta-Lien or Dairen. St. Petersburg also gained Chinese permission to build a 700-mile spur of the Chinese Eastern Railway southwestwards from Harbin to Port Arthur. From the South Manchurian Railway, as this spur was known, branch lines could quickly be constructed to the Korean border.

In April 1898, the Japanese gave tacit recognition to the Russian lease of Port Arthur in exchange for a free hand in Korea. But the Russian concessions on the Korean island of Ullung (Dagelet) and in the Sea of Japan, as well as the Russian attempt to obtain facilities on Choryong Island, remained major irritants. The Russians also had ambitions of gaining a naval base near Masan, thirty miles west of Pusan. It became impossible for Japan to ignore the strategic implications of Russian aspirations in Korea.

The balance seemed to tip even further against Japan in the aftermath of the Boxer rebellion in north China during 1900–01. An international army was sent to Peking to suppress this anti-foreign rising; under the pretext of guarding their railway concessions the Russians dispatched over 150,000 troops to Manchuria. These forces remained in the area despite an agreement with the Chinese in early 1902 to withdraw. In the early months of 1903, Russian forces crossed the lower Yalu estuary and occupied Korean territory at Yongampo. This was done without any authorization or concession from the Korean government.

By this time, the balance of power had begun to swing in Japan's favor. The Japanese army and navy had been significantly expanded since 1895 and the Japanese economy continued to thrive. The Anglo-Japanese treaty of 30 January 1902 was also of great significance. The treaty tended to isolate Russia in the Far East, gave Japan a great-power ally, and implicitly demonstrated that the Western maritime powers were concerned over Russian objectives in Manchuria and Korea. The treaty specifically recognized that Korea lay within the Japanese sphere of influence.

As the first Russian troop reinforcements for Manchuria came over the newly-opened Trans-Siberian railway in early 1903, it became obvious that the long-prophesied confrontation between Russia and Japan was at hand. Formal negotiations between the two adversaries opened in August 1903 as both sides stepped up their preparations for war.

While the Russians demanded exclusive control of Manchuria, they were prepared to give Japan a free hand south of the 39th Parallel in Korea. Japan counter-proposed with a plan for a neutral zone along the Korean-Manchurian border, thus completely excluding Russian influence from Korea. The two positions over Korea could not be reconciled and there was a complete impasse.

Japan now turned from diplomacy to war, breaking off negotiations on 6 February 1904. Two days later Japanese warships attacked the Russian fleet in Port Arthur; hostilities were declared on the 10th. The Times of London considered that "The Japanese Navy has opened the war by an act of daring which is destined to take a place of honor in naval annals."

With great speed, Japan also transported an expeditionary force to Inchon. Seoul was occupied, and the Korean government forced to give Japan complete freedom of military action in Korea. All Russian concessions in Korea were taken over by Japan. The Japanese also took over all telegraph lines within Korea, and appointed advisers to all Korean ministries. Meanwhile, Russian scouting parties from Manchuria were probing deep into northern Korea.

From Inchon Japanese forces marched northwards to the Yalu and onwards into Manchuria to besiege Port Arthur, which eventually surrendered with its large garrison in January 1905.

The loss of this great fortress was of course a major setback for the Russians. The fall of Port Arthur was soon followed by the Japanese defeat of the main Russian Far Eastern armies at Mukden, southern Manchuria, after a prolonged 17-day battle during February and March 1905. At sea the Russian Baltic Fleet, which had been sent round the world, was almost entirely sunk in Japan's classic naval victory near Tsushima Island in the Korea Strait on 27 May 1905.

These historic victories made Japan a world power and gave it a regional ascendancy in North East Asia that was to last for forty years. The fate of Korea for the next four decades was also decided by these Japanese successes and the Treaty of Portsmouth, New Hampshire (5 September 1905), which ratified Japan's victory.

By this treaty Japan acquired the Russian lease of Port Arthur, Dairen, and the Liaotung Peninsula. Japan was also awarded the Russian-built South Manchurian Railway from Port Arthur northwards to Changchun, which cemented the Japanese hold on southern Manchuria. Japan also won southern Sakhalin, the Russian island to the north of the Japanese home island of Hokkaido.

The Treaty of Portsmouth formally gave Japan a free hand in Korea, for the accord specifically acknowledged that Russia accepted Japan's "paramount political, military and economic interest in Korea."

It was in this way that the Russo-Japanese rivalry over Korea was finally resolved. Only five years of token independence now remained to Korea before final, formal annexation by Japan.

The Road to Annexation

During the Russo-Japanese war, Japan had assumed military control in Korea. The Japanese were particularly sensitive about the main railway and its associated telegraph system, which ran from Pusan in southeast Korea through Seoul to Pyongyang and the Yalu. Along this line, men and supplies were sent from the homeland to sustain Japan's armies in Manchuria. A major link in the system was the 3,000-foot long Yalu highway bridge, built in 1900, which joined Sinuiju in Korea with Antung in Manchuria.

Korea was thus strategically indispensable to the maintenance of the new Japanese civil and military presence in Manchuria following Russia's defeat. It became of great importance to the Japanese government to legitimize Japan's ever-growing interests in Korea, both internationally and with the weak Korean government. Thus, even before the Portsmouth treaty of September 1905, Japan obtained American and British recognition of its vital interests in Korea.

On 29 July 1905, during a visit to Tokyo, the American Secretary of State, William H. Taft, concluded a secret agreement with the Japanese Premier, Count Katsura. In this agreement, the United States approved Japan's "suzerainty over Korea" in exchange for a pledge that Japan did not harbor any designs against the Philippines. It will be remembered that these islands had fallen to the United States after the Spanish-American War of 1898.

A few days later on 12 August 1905, the Anglo-Japanese Treaty of Alliance was renewed. In exchange for an understanding that Japan would not in any way threaten Singapore, Great Britain recognized Japan's "paramount" political, military, and economic interests in Korea. For the Western powers generally, a Japanese-controlled Korea was preferable to Russian influence in that country. Together with the Treaty of Portsmouth, therefore, these Japanese agreements with Britain and America ended the period of intense international rivalry in East Asia and restored a balance of power.

Japan also moved quickly to obtain official Korean recognition of its dominant presence within the peninsula. A draft Protectorate Treaty was presented to the Korean government during October 1905. This proposed treaty delegated Korea's foreign relations to Japanese control, so precluding any independent Korean diplomatic initiatives. A Japanese Resident-General in Seoul would supervise the protectorate; Japanese regional commissioners, acting under the Resident-General, would be placed in the Korean provinces. The Korean Emperor, Kojong, would have his safety guaranteed by the Japanese and would continue to reign; but much of the essence of Korean sovereignty would pass to Japan.

The Protectorate Treaty was debated by a Korean government surrounded by troops from the Japanese garrison in Seoul, and was eventually signed by both sides on 17 November 1905. The veteran Meiji statesman, Ito Hirobumi, became the first Japanese Resident-General. He was responsible to the Japanese Emperor and had the authority to use Japanese troops to enforce his powers. Apart from one battalion for the Korean Emperor's security, the Korean army was dissolved. Korea thus became a Japanese protectorate.

As might be expected, the Protectorate Treaty aroused much opposition in Korea. The Japanese military presence was underlined by the increasing number of Japanese colonists and settlers who flocked to Korea and who were now allowed to buy land. The Emperor Kojong made an attempt to alert world opinion to this gradual process of Japanese colonization. In early 1907, the Emperor sent a secret mission to the Second International Peace Conference held at The Hague in the Netherlands.

Although the mission failed to obtain an official hearing there was a strong Japanese response. Kojong was forced to abdicate in July 1907. He was succeeded by the Crown Prince, the last monarch of the Yi dynasty, who was later given the posthumous title of Sunjong. In a further effort to strengthen their position in Korea, the Japanese imposed the "New Agreement" on an already subservient Korean government. The Japanese Resident-General took fresh powers, senior Japanese officials were inserted into the Korean government, and the Korean Army was finally abolished.

These new Japanese measures were implemented against a background of widespread Korean resistance. Armed clashes and attacks on Japanese garrisons and communications developed into guerrilla operations on a national scale. Many Korean villages were destroyed and there were, of course, many Korean casualties. But as the Korean insurgents found it hard to obtain arms, resistance was gradually beaten down between 1907 and 1910. In Japan, meanwhile, there were demands for the outright annexation of Korea.

Yet as Korean independence came to an end in these unhappy circumstances, the indigenous process of cultural and educational renaissance continued. John K. Fairbank has written that "it was particularly tragic that the Korean people, having come at last into contact with the modern world, should be so soon subjugated by Asia's first leader in modernization, Japan. . . . Korean nationhood was thus suppressed at the very time when conservative *yangban* . . . reformist students, disbanded soldiers, and impoverished peasants, rebelling alike against foreign rule, were developing a common sentiment of nationalism. . . ." Future events were to show that this new spirit of Korean nationalism was to flourish steadily under Japanese rule.

The final act of the annexation process began with the assassination of Ito Hirobumi by a young Korean patriot at Harbin, Manchuria, in October 1909. Shortly before, Ito had resigned in favor of Sone Atasuke as the Japanese Resident-General in Korea. But upon Ito's death, a former Japanese War Minister, General Terauchi Masatake, was now made Resident-General in Korea. In early 1910, General Terauchi placed the Japanese civil police in Korea under the control of the military police. A draft Annexation Treaty was presented to an intimidated Korean government.

Eventually the Korean-Japanese Annexation Treaty was signed on 22 August 1910. It provided for all treaties between Japan and other countries to apply to Korea; all treaties signed by Korea were to be voided. The Korean Emperor Sunjong was reduced to the rank of king and pensioned off. Korea was to be ruled by a new Japanese agency, the Chosen Government-General, which took its name from the ancient name of Korea.

On 29 August 1910, the Annexation Treaty came into force, and on that day both the rule of the Yi dynasty and Korean independence came to an end. Korea was now to remain a Japanese colony until the moment of Japan's defeat in the Second World War.

Korean Resistance Fighters against the Japanese.

An Chong-gun, Assassin of Ito Hirobumi, making a Political Statement.

CHAPTER 7

JAPANESE RULE 1910–1945

Many East Asian countries were affected by the colonial experience. But Korea was unique in that it was formally ruled from August 1910 to August 1945 by an Asian neighbor with which cultural and historical links had always been close. As we have seen earlier in our story it was through Korea that Chinese writing, religion, and art forms reached Japan. But in general these cultural contacts counted for little during the period of Japanese rule, which paradoxically was a period of both cultural repression and administrative innovation.

Following the Annexation Treaty of August 1910, the new Chosen Government-General acted quickly to impose its authority. The chief security agency of Japanese rule remained the military police (or gendarmerie), which as we have seen had authority over the civil police. But since about 1906, a division of Japanese regular troops had been stationed in Korea, a force that was increased to two divisions in 1915.

The gendarmerie, which recruited Koreans, operated throughout the country. The Japanese army, meanwhile, suppressed the remaining Korean guerrilla bands in the northern part of the country. But these partisans were never completely eliminated until towards the end of the Japanese rule, for they made good use of local knowledge and also of the Chinese and Russian borders for their protection.

In general the Japanese were to claim that their rule brought efficiency, as well as reform to the Korean administration. The Government-General functioned as an autonomous organization under the Colonial Ministry until 1942, when Korea was administered as part of Japan under the Home Ministry. Ultimately all major decrees had to be sanctioned by the Emperor, and the Imperial Diet in Tokyo held oversight on policy matters including finance. But within these parameters, the Governor-General had broad executive powers both civil and military. He appointed all officials except his chief assistant, the Administrative Director, who was appointed by the Imperial Government.

Japanese Administration and Economic Policy

The more general activities of Japanese government in Korea were carried out by a small number of ministries such as those dealing with Finance, Home Affairs, Justice, Agriculture, and Industry. The Governor-General's Administrative Director headed a powerful executive Secretariat, which was comprised of more specialized bureaus or sections. These included Police, Railways, the Land Survey, Trading Monopolies, and so on. A Japanese local government system was established from the province level down through prefectures to townships and villages. All senior and middle-level officials were invariably Japanese.

Japanese government in Korea was therefore comprehensive, but historians of their rule have noted that Japanese administration was not simply a matter of law and order. There was a distinct element of cultural regimentation, for as an ancient people the Koreans saw their language and history as rallying points against foreign rule. Thus Japanese was enforced as the language of government and education, a Japanese press was set up in each Korean province, and the Japanese renamed some Korean cities and towns. The Korean press and publishing were carefully censored. All Korean political groupings were banned. Through these and other measures, the Japanese attempted to enforce a policy of cultural assimilation between Japan and Korea.

During the first two decades of Japanese rule, until about 1931, the primary objective of economic policy lay in the development of the agricultural sector. Japanese settlers flocked to Korea, and the Japanese-owned Oriental Development Company was at the forefront of an almost classic example of colonial exploitation.

Initially, the Japanese encountered a significant problem in their attempts to expand Korean agriculture as a source of cheap food for the homeland. Traditional Korean farming was inefficient, and usually organized on a local basis. Large areas of land were loosely attached to the estates of the former Korean royal family or to senior *yangban* estates. There were further ill-defined areas of common land. The Japanese therefore initiated in the first years of their rule, a comprehensive land survey on a national scale. The survey attempted to define the precise ownership of Korean land with a view to development in the interests of the new rulers of Korea.

Many Korean peasants, as well as small tenant farmers, who tended their land by custom either failed to register or could not prove title in the Western sense. Large areas of land thus lapsed by law to the Government-General, which now came to own about five percent of cultivated land. Other land was conveyed to the Government in lieu of unpaid taxes. The Japanese administration of Korea thus became a major landlord in its own right. Some of this land was leased to Japanese individuals, but the Government-General also used the Oriental Development Company as its agent in developing its newly-acquired estates.

Consolidation of forfeited land in this way made for a certain degree of efficiency. The Japanese pursued modern measures of agricultural improvement, sponsoring irrigation and drainage schemes, and the intensive use of fertilizers. The administrative framework of Korean agriculture was modernized, and thus land came to be used more efficiently. Production of rice and other cereals rose significantly, but at the cost of driving many impoverished Koreans from the land to the cities and towns. Other Koreans emigrated to Manchuria.

By the early 1930s, it had been calculated that Korean rice production had increased by about one-third since 1910. But about one-half of this total was being exported to Japan, so that Korean per capita consumption of rice had declined by over forty percent over the same period, allowing for the increase in the Korean population. This process of enforced decline in the rice consumption, and hence of the basic standard of living, was one of the major complaints against Japanese rule in Korea. Another charge against the economic policies of the Government-General was its creation of official trading monopolies that closed down Korean firms, so precluding the development of Korean capital.

On the other hand, there was a considerable and systematic expansion of public works under Japanese rule. New roads,

Rice awaiting shipment to Japan from Inch'on Harbor.

railways, bridges, harbors, schools, and hospitals were built, often for military or strategic reasons. Communications were improved. Public health measures on a significant level were introduced. Between 1910 and 1945, the Korean population doubled. After 1931, once again for strategic reasons, which we shall note below, a certain amount of industrial development took place in Korea. In many ways, Korea was transformed during the thirty-five years of Japanese rule.

From the earliest days of Japanese administration, national aspirations for lost independence counted for more than any purely economic balance sheet. Both countries shared a Confucian heritage. But imposed change and modernization were suspect because they were associated with alien rule.

The Korean Independence Movement

On 1 March 1919, there were nation-wide mass demonstrations in support of Korean independence. For several years before this date a mass protest against Japanese rule had been discussed amongst a diverse group: exiled Koreans in China and Manchuria, Korean students in Japan, and patriots within Korea itself. This latter group included Buddhist organizations and the *Chondo-gyo* ("The Society of the Heavenly Way"), the successor to the *Tonghak* movement of the late nineteenth century.

In particular, the independence movement was also inspired by the right of national self-determination proclaimed in President Woodrow Wilson's "Fourteen Points" for a just settlement of the First World War. The movement was thus broadly based and fully conscious of events in the Western world. The new Korean nationalism, rather than looking backwards to the Confucian monarchy, thus envisaged a modern, independent democratic state.

Early in 1919, a Declaration of Korean Independence was drafted and secretly circulated throughout Korea. The movement was sponsored on the national level by 33 leading Koreans, and by local supporters in other parts of the country. On 1 March 1919, the 33 leaders read the "Declaration" in Seoul. The Declaration was also publicly read throughout Korea: "We herewith proclaim the independence of Korea . . . in witness of the equality of all nations, and we pass it on to our posterity as their inherent right. . . . The result of annexation, brought about against the will of the Korean people, is that the Japanese are concerned only for their own gain. . . ." Two million people throughout Korea are believed to have taken part in the subsequent demonstrations.

These mass demonstrations were, of course, suppressed with a great severity that is still recalled; but the 1 March protest involved Koreans of all classes and viewpoints and thus intensified a common awareness of shared nationality. The demonstrations, which showed to world opinion the nature of Japanese rule in Korea, also resulted in some practical reforms. The Japanese created a Central Advisory Council, composed of Koreans, and also set up a parallel system of provincial and local advisory councils. Some members of these councils were elected on a restricted franchise. The military gendarmerie was replaced by a civilian police. Controls over the Korean press and publishing were relaxed. These limited reforms also reflected a period of liberalism in Japan; some upper class and affluent Koreans were won over to the government in this way.

Main Hall of Chondo-gyo Temple in Seoul.

The Declaration of Independence (1 March 1919).

Koreans In Exile

However, the fundamental nature of Japanese colonial rule remained unchanged. Hence the demonstrations of 1 March 1919 signified the beginning of a new struggle for Korean independence, not only within Korea but also abroad. Perhaps the most visible result of the movement was the establishment of a Korean Provisional Government-in-exile in the French concession of Shanghai on 18 September 1919. This government was formed by representatives from Korean groups in Manchuria, Siberia, and China.

The first President of the Provisional Government was the veteran nationalist Syngman Rhee, whose prestige was probably higher than any other Korean exile. Following the suppression of the Independence Club in 1898, Rhee had been imprisoned for seven years by the Korean government. On his release, he had gone to America where he had studied at Harvard and received a doctorate from Princeton in 1910. Rhee had then returned to Korea in the early years of Japanese rule, but had understandably gone into exile again. He now made his home in Hawaii, where there was a Korean community, until the 1930s.

Like so many exiled political groups, the Korean Provisional Government was soon splintered by irreconcilable policy differences. One faction advocated direct military action against Japan, while another favored long-term propaganda aimed at the Korean homeland. Syngman Rhee, as befitted his American background, favored political work and lobbying in the United States, which was now emerging as Japan's main strategic rival in the Pacific area.

Syngman Rhee.

During the early 1920s, therefore, Rhee set up in Washington the Korean Commission, which was in effect a shadow legation of the Provisional Government. Rhee soon became estranged from the operations of the exiled Government, which now came under the leadership of another well-known Korean expatriate, Kim Ku. Rhee continued to regard himself as President of the Provisional Government. He continued to work in his own way for Korean independence in Hawaii and in the United States.

The exiles that supported the generally conservative Korean Provisional Government represented only part of the Korean community abroad. Koreans in Siberia had formed Communist and Socialist groups as early as 1918–19, under the influence of the Russian Revolution. In January 1921, a Korean Communist Party was formed in Shanghai; but Lenin soon decided that the Communist International (or Comintern) could not recognize a Korean Party that was based outside Korea. As a result, Korean communist groups from Siberia, Shanghai, and Tokyo established a new, underground Korean Communist Party in Seoul in April 1925. The party was affiliated to the Comintern, and thus part of the international Communist movement.

The Party was bedeviled by disunity and by the activity of the Japanese police from its very inception. In December 1928, the Comintern dissolved the party for factionalism and ineffectiveness. A few Korean Communists remained to work underground until 1945, but most of the leadership escaped to Siberia, Manchuria, or China. From 1927 to about 1931, an alliance of Communists and Korean Nationalists existed in the "New Korea Society" (the *Shinganhoe*). But this group too was eventually dissolved because of its own disunity and the intense surveillance of the police. Thus by the early 1930s, the internal Korean independence movement had been neutralized or liquidated by the Japanese.

Despite these setbacks within Korea, the cause of Korean independence continued to flourish in radically new settings. Some of the Korean Communists who had fled to China entered the Chinese Communist Party and eventually, after 1935, reached Mao Tse-tung's Yenan headquarters in north China. Here these Koreans later formed a Korean Independence League, as well as a small Korean Volunteer Army of several hundred men that fought alongside the Chinese Communists against the Japanese until 1945.

Other Korean Communists in Manchuria also fought with the Chinese Communists in the 1930s. These Koreans operated both in eastern Manchuria and across the international border in northeast Korea. Eventually the Japanese military pushed these insurgents into Soviet Siberia in 1941. One of these Korean guerrillas was named Kim Sung Chu, who took the name of Kim Il Sung, a celebrated anti-Japanese fighter of an earlier generation. Kim Il Sung's precise links with the Soviets after 1941 have never been elucidated, but what is certain is that he returned to Korea with the Soviet Army in 1945. He then began an entirely new chapter in Korean history as the Soviet-backed leader of Communist North Korea.

While these different cadres of Korean Communists fought with Mao's armies, the Korean Provisional Government under Kim Ku as its President, remained in Shanghai until the Japanese invasion of China in 1937. The Provisional Government then fled in stages before the Japanese to Chungking, deep in the

The Korean Independence Army.

Chinese interior, which was Chiang Kai-shek's wartime capital. Here in Chungking, Kim Ku formed a Korean unit to fight with the Chinese Nationalists; the Korean Provisional Government declared war against Japan after the Pearl Harbor attack of 7 December 1941. But as we shall see, official recognition by the United States, or indeed any other country, eluded these Koreans in Nationalist China.

Syngman Rhee, meanwhile, had continued to work for Korean independence without much success. He had tried, in vain, to present the case for independence to the League of Nations in Geneva in 1932, when that body discussed the Japanese seizure of Manchuria. Rhee had then made several lecture tours in the United States. Eventually, late in the 1930s, Rhee left Hawaii to live in Washington, and to wait for what he considered would be the inevitable war between Japan and the United States. From then until 1945, Syngman Rhee was to term himself the Chairman of the Korean Commission in the United States. But this rather grand title carried little if any influence in Washington.

We can thus see from these events that the wide ideological, personal, and geographical differences within the Korean Independence movement precluded the formation of a unified, effective government-in-exile. During the 1930s, moreover, Korea had become ever more integrated within the strategic and economic administration of the Japanese Empire as the Rising Sun spread into the whole of Manchuria, north China, and then deep into China proper.

Thus by the late 1930s, the one belief shared by the far-flung members of the different Korean independence movements was the conviction that only the military defeat of Imperial Japan would bring freedom to Korea.

Japanese Rule: The Final Phase

In September 1931, following an incident at Mukden between Chinese and Japanese troops, Japan began the occupation of the whole of Manchuria. The following year, the puppet state of Manchukuo was set up: the Japanese soon moved into the neighboring Chinese province of Jehol. These were successive steps in an expansionist drive that was to lead Japan into full-scale conflict in China by 1937. After a further four years of ever-increasing tension in the Far East, Japan went to war with the United States and the British Empire in December 1941.

These historic events had a very important effect on Korea. After 1931 the relative relaxation of controls that had characterized Japanese policy in Korea during the 1920s was reversed as Japan began to put its continental possessions on a war footing. Increasing emphasis was given to strategic industrial investment in both Korea and Manchuria. The stress on agricultural development in Korea, which had characterized the first two decades of Japanese rule, was downgraded. A new priority was given to improving communications, and especially those between Korea and Manchuria. In line with this latter policy, a new double-tracked railway bridge was built over the Yalu between Sinuiju and Antung in Manchuria, a link that was claimed to be the longest railway bridge in the Japanese Empire.

As an integral part of this program, the mining of coal, iron, and other non-ferrous minerals found in northern Korea was stepped up. Some metal processing and chemical plants were built, mostly in northeast Korea where the ports of Hungnam and Chongjin gave easy access by sea to Japan, so cutting production and transportation overheads. A small iron and steel industry was developed in northern Korea, as well as facilities for manufacturing machine tools. Light industry was promoted around Seoul and Pyongyang.

From 1931 to 1941, manufacturing as a share of the total Korean national product increased from 20 percent to 40 percent. During the period of Japanese rule as a whole, the agricultural labor force dropped from 90 percent of the total in 1910 to about 70 percent in the early 1940s.

The showpiece of Japanese industrial development in Korea was the hydroelectric industry, which was planned to mobilize the potential energy resources of Korea's northern rivers. Large facilities were built at Changjin (in Japanese, Chosin), north of Hungnam, and at nearby Pujon (Fusen). At Suiho on the Yalu River, about sixty miles upstream from Sinuiju, Japanese engineers constructed the 3,000-foot long Supung dam with a large power house on the Korean side of the river. The Suiho plant provided power for much of Korea and also for the industrial zone of southern Manchuria.

This partial Japanese industrialization of Korea in the 1930s has to be seen in its historical context. Following the launching of the "China Incident" in 1937, the industrial targets of the Korean economy were controlled as part of the "Japan-Korea-Manchuria Resources Mobilization Plan." The Imperial Japanese Planning Board set the targets for Korea, and the whole concept of continental development under Japanese aegis was rationalized in late

1938, when Japan proclaimed the "New Order in East Asia." The region was to become self-sufficient, and Western influences excluded. When Japan turned south during 1940–41, the concept of the "New Order" was naturally succeeded by that of the "Greater East Asia Co-Prosperity Sphere."

Korea's role in this hegemonistic strategy was central. By the late 1930s, the peninsula was becoming a virtual Japanese military base both by reason of its growing industrial resources and its strategic geographical position between Japan and Manchuria.

The industrial, manpower, and natural assets of Korea were increasingly seen as elements in a war economy, which after 1941 was now organized on a totalitarian basis. All Korean industrial production not needed for Japanese military purposes was curtailed. The corollary was that Korean agriculture was even further downgraded as Korea became increasingly integrated into the Japanese war economy. Koreans were conscripted into the Japanese army, and after 1939 drafted for forced labor as well.

As part of this integration process, the administrative links between the two countries became ever closer. After thirty years of autonomous administration within the Japanese Empire, the coming of the Pacific War in December 1941 meant that Korea was now completely subordinated in its government to Japan.

During 1942 it was decreed that Korea would be governed by the Japanese Home Affairs Ministry, with the administration in Seoul acting as its agent. The following year, the police system was reorganized. By 1945 there were over 300,000 Japanese troops garrisoned in Korea. Korea was thus ruled as part of Japan.

In the wake of this administrative integration, the process of enforced cultural assimilation between the two countries came to its climax. The last two Korean-language newspapers had been closed in 1940, and it was even decreed in the final years of Japan's rule that Koreans should take Japanese personal names. In early 1945 the Japanese announced a plan for the election of 10 Korean representatives to the Upper House of the Diet in Tokyo, and for the election of 16 Korean representatives to the Lower House. This was the culmination of the wartime integration process termed "Japan and Korea One Body" (*Naisen Ittai*).

This plan for integrating the two countries on the legislative level was of course never implemented. By early 1945, Japan's military position was already desperate. When the two atomic bombs were dropped on Hiroshima and Nagasaki on 6 and 9 August 1945, total defeat was imminent. With the Imperial Rescript announcing Japan's capitulation on 15 August 1945, Korea was freed from Japanese rule under terms of the Cairo and Potsdam declarations, which Japan had accepted with its surrender.

In retrospect the period of Japanese rule is one of complicated paradox. Loss of Korean independence was accompanied by an intensive modernization process in some key sectors of the Korean economy. Undeniable economic exploitation by Japan, especially in the agricultural sector, was balanced by the deliberate creation, often for strategic reasons, of the public works and communications infrastructure of a modern country.

For the same strategic reasons the Korean economy was partly industrialized after 1931. When Japan acknowledged defeat in August 1945, Korea was further along the road towards modernization than any other Asian country apart from Japan itself. But the cost to Koreans had been heavy.

Perhaps the greatest paradox of all lay in the circumstances that surrounded the ending of Japan's rule in Korea. For at the very moment of capitulation, Korea was partitioned for the first time since the emergence of the Silla Kingdom.

EPILOGUE

In recent times, since 1945, North Korea has remained a closed society. South Korea, on the other hand, has sometimes attracted world attention through increasingly vocal demands for internal reform. It should be remembered, however, that South Korea has faced very great adversities in the past generation. Following the destruction of the Korean War, the economy remained very weak for a decade, unable to sustain an attempt at parliamentary government during 1960–61.

Following a military coup in 1961, South Korea enjoyed both political stability and economic growth that, within twenty years, turned the ROK into an advanced industrial country. But as the ROK's prosperity grew, so did expectations of a more democratic form of government. These expectations culminated in the student riots and other disturbances in the summer of 1987.

South Korea's leaders then wisely bowed to the inevitable. On 29 June 1987, Mr. Roh Tae Woo, the Presidential candidate of the ruling Democratic Justice Party (DJP), announced his support for wide-ranging reforms that included direct presidential elections. A few days later, President Chun Doo Hwan endorsed these proposed reforms and stated that South Korea would now achieve "an advanced form of democracy that we can proudly show the world."

Since then solid progress has been made in drafting a new constitution. In August 1987, it was reported that agreement between the ruling and opposition parties had been reached on direct presidential elections. A national referendum then decisively approved these constitutional provisions in October 1987. In the elections on 16 December 1987, Roh Tae Woo was elected President of the ROK. There is every hope for a new democratic structure in South Korea—and continuing improved relations with the North.

*Summit Meeting between North and South Korean Leaders at
Pyongyang. June 15, 2000.*

INDEX

Note: italics denote illustrations, pictures and maps

Forthcoming Illustrated Histories from Hippocrene Books

FALL 2000

France: An Illustrated History
Lisa Neal

Encompassing more than 500,000 years from primordial times to the 21st century, French history is a vast body run through by manifold and, often turbulent, currents. This volume provides a succinct panorama of these cultural, political, and social currents, as well as concise analyses of their origins and effects. Complemented by 50 illustrations and maps, this text is an invaluable addition to the library of the traveler, the student, and the history enthusiast.

150 pages • 5 X 7 • 50 b/w photos/illus./maps • $14.95hc • 0-7818-0835-9 • W • (105)

Poland: An Illustrated History
Iwo Cyprian Pogonowski

Poland's remarkable quest for representative government, the oldest in modern Europe, is presented against the backdrop of a millennium of history rich in cultural, political, and social events. These topics—complemented with Polish art, literature, music, architecture, and traditions—are knowlededgably described in this concise volume, which further offers more than 50 photos, illustrations, and maps.

150 pages • 5 X 7 • 50 b/w photos/illus./maps • $14.95hc • 0-7818-0757-3• W • (404)

Spain: An Illustrated History

Fred James Hill

This concise, illustrated history explores the remarkable history of Spain—a thriving center of Islamic civilization until its eventual conquest by Catholic kings—from the first millennium B.C. to the 21st century. With its succinct portrayal of the country's political and social history, along with the concomitant cultural developments and achievements, this volume is perfect for the traveler, student, and history enthusiast.

150 pages • 5 X 7 • 50 b/w photos/illus./maps
• $14.95hc • 0-7818-0836-7 • W • (113)

Other Illustrated Histories from Hippocrene Books . . .

The Celtic World: An Illustrated History

Patrick Lavin

From the valleys of Bronze Age Urnfielders to the works of 20th century Irish-American literary greats Mary Higgins Clark and Seamus Heaney, Patrick Lavin guides the reader on an entertaining and informative journey through 182 captivating pages of Celtic history, culture, and tradition. Complemented by 50 illustrations and maps, this concise yet insightful survey is a convenient reference guide for both the traveler and scholar.

185 pages • 5 x 7 • 50 b/w illus./maps
• $14.95hc • 0-7818-0731-X • W • (582)

China: An Illustrated History
Yong Ho

China is one of the oldest civilizations in the world, with a recorded history that spans almost 4,000 years; yet, to much of the outside world, it remains a mystery. This concise, illustrated volume offers the reader a panoramic view of this remarkable land, from its remote antiquity to the 21st century.

142 pages • 5 x 7 • 50 b/w illus./maps
• $14.95hc • 0-7818-0821-9 • W • (542)

England: An Illustrated History
Henry Weisser

English history is a rich and complex subject that has had a major influence upon the development of the language, laws, institutions, practices and ideas of the United States and many other countries throughout the world. Just how did all of this originate over the centuries in this pleasant, green kingdom? This concise, illustrated volume traces the story from England's most distant past to the present day, highlighting important political and social developments as well as cultural achievements.

166 pages • 5 x 7 • 50 b/w illus./maps
• $11.95hc • 0-7818-0751-4 • W • (446)

Ireland: An Illustrated History
Henry Weisser

Erin go bragh! While it is easy to appreciate the natural beauty of Ireland, the Emerald Isle's history is also a rich and complex subject of study. Spanning prehistoric and Celtic Ireland to modern times, this concise, illustrated volume examines the people, religion, social changes, and politics that have evolved into the tradition of modern Ireland.

166 pages • 5 x 7 • 50 b/w illus./maps
• $11.95hc • 0-7818-0693-3 • W • (782)

Israel: An Illustrated History

David C. Gross

Israel has always been a major player on the world stage. This concise, illustrated volume offers the reader an informative, panoramic view of this remarkable land, from biblical days to the 21st century. With topics exploring art, literature, sculpture, music, science, politics, religion and more, here is a wonderful gift book for travelers, students, or anyone seeking to expand their knowledge of Israeli history, culture, and heritage.

160 pages • 5 x 7 • 50 b/w illus./maps
• $11.95hc • 0-7818-0756-5 • W • (24)

Italy: An Illustrated History

Joseph F. Privitera

"A history shorn of a country's cultural element is not a true history of its people." This illustrated history adheres to the above line that opens it. Written in an accessible style, it covers the full panoply of Italy's history—from Roman times to the 21st century—and includes concise accounts of the major political, military, and cultural events that have shaped the country over the centuries.

142 pages • 5 x 7 • 50 b/w illus./maps
• $14.95hc • 0-7818-0819-4 • W • (436)

Mexico: An Illustrated History

Michael Burke

This convenient historical guide traces Mexico from the peasant days of the Olmecs to the late 20th century. With over 150 pages and 50 illustrations, the reader discovers how events of Mexico's past have left an indelible mark on the politics, economy, culture, spirit, and growth of this country and its people.

183 pages • 5 x 7 • 50 b/w illus.

• $11.95hc • 0-7818-0690-9 • W • (585)

Poland in World War II: An Illustrated Military History

Andrew Hempel

This illustrated history is a concise presentation of the Polish military war effort in World War II, intermingled with factual human-interest stories and 50 black-and-white photos and illustrations.

117 pages • 5 x 7 • 50 b/w illus.

• $11.95hc • 0-7818-0758-1 • W • (541)

Russia: An Illustrated History

Joel Carmichael

Encompassing one-sixth of the earth's land surface—the equivalent of the whole North American continent—Russia is the largest country in the world. Renowned historian Joel Carmichael presents Russia's rich and expansive past—upheaval, reform, social change, growth—in an easily accessible and concentrated

volume. From the Tatar's reign to modern-day Russia, the book spans seven centuries of cultural, social and political events.
252 pages • 5 x 7 • 50 b/w illus.
• $14.95hc • 0-7818-0689-5 • W • (781)

Prices subject to change without notice. **To purchase Hippocrene Books** contact your local bookstore, call (718) 454-2366, or write to: HIPPOCRENE BOOKS, 171 Madison Avenue, New York, NY 10016. Please enclose check or money order, adding $5.00 shipping (UPS) for the first book and $.50 for each additional book.